LAMBTON

An Illustrated History of the County

LAMBTON

An Illustrated History of the County

Glen C. Phillips

CHESHIRE CAT PRESS

Sarnia   Ontario   Canada

Cheshire Cat Press
Box 2611, Sarnia, Ontario
N7T 7V8   519-472-5572

Printed in Canada by
Ampersand Printing
Guelph, Ontario

Canadian Cataloguing in Publication Data
Phillips, Glen Christopher, 1967-

Lambton: an illustrated history of the county

Includes index.
ISBN 0-921818-20-3

1. Lambton (Ont.) - History.   2. Lambton (Ont.) - History - Pictorial works.
I. Title

FC3095.L36P48 1999   971.3'27   C99-930872-6
F1059.L23P44 1999

This is book number _1720_ of a limited
first edition of 2,000 copies.

CONTENTS

6   *Preface & Acknowledgements*

7   *Introduction*

8   *The Emergence of a County*

16   *Townships*

26   *Streetscapes*

36   *Government & Public Life*

44   *Daily Life in a Different Age*

51   *Tipplers & Teetotallers*

58   *Agriculture*

65   *Commerce*

73   *Industry*

81   *Wealth from Beneath the Soil*

89   *Portside*

98   *Getting Around*

106   *Sports & Recreation*

114   *Disasters, Mishaps & Criminal Acts*

123   *Patrons*

124   *Index*

PREFACE & ACKNOWLEDGEMENTS

While taking university history courses, I was told by some of my professors that the historian should approach and write about his or her topic without any bias or emotion. Well, since I could be a rather poor student at times, I never managed to learn this lesson. History is about people, and people are about passion. So, how could one possibly look at the past as if one were observing some mundane chemical reaction taking place in a test tube? I, for one, cannot. Perhaps, I did learn something nonetheless. At any rate, I hope that readers will discover that this work of history bubbles with enthusiasm. I further hope that readers will recognize that I approached my subject with a certain amount of bias. Quite simply, I'll always hold Lambton near to my heart because it is my home county. For me, it was a great place in which to grow up.

Writing this book has been quite difficult. Yes, I've had the usual wrestling matches with the computer – which the blasted machine usually won – and I've had some fairly trying times tracking down obscure historical facts buried in musty old archival sources. However, these problems are par for the course and haven't made things too hard. While it may seem strange at first, what truly has made this project difficult is my love for Lambton. You see, if anything, this book is a good-bye of sorts. At the end of this year, I'll be joining my wife, Crystal, to build a new life together in Dublin, Ireland. It's a big step for both of us, but one that is filled with exciting possibilities. Still, it's never easy to leave one's home. Of course, I'll always return for visits, and I also plan to re-visit Lambton's history in the future. After all, the county has so many fascinating stories that beg to be told.

Naturally, all of those who helped me with this project made my job much easier by providing research materials and many of the historical images which appear in the book. For their dedicated assistance, I would like to thank Donna McGuire of the Oil Museum of Canada, Laurie Mason of Moore Museum, the late Maude Dalgety and Glenda Young of Sombra Township Museum, John Lutman and Theresa Regnier of the J.J. Talman Regional Collection, Allan Day of the Surveyor General's Office, and the staffs at the Sarnia Public Library, the City of Toronto Archives, the D.B. Weldon Library, the Archives of Ontario, the National Library of Canada, and the National Archives of Canada. In particular, I would like to express my heartfelt appreciation to Anne Ashton, Lorraine Thompson, and Helen Maddock of the Lambton Room, and to Paul Miller, formerly of Lambton Heritage Museum. Over the past year or so, these professionals have unselfishly spent countless hours helping me with this book. Also, I would like to acknowledge the contributions of Laura Babcock, Gene Buell, Hugo Holland, and Shirley Dudley of the Lambton Mutual Insurance Company. They cheerfully loaned me items and shared their love of the past with me. In addition, Alan Noon deserves credit for his photographic skill and all the timely copy work he did for me.

By the way, I can state with absolute confidence that this is the only local history book about a Canadian place that was mostly written in Dublin. In between pints of that nectar of the gods, Guinness, I wrote about two-thirds of the following pages during a six-week visit to that city earlier this year. On this score, I would like to thank Paddy and Graínne O'Flynn of Leinster Road for generously allowing me access to their computer and all those great jazz CDs. Finally, my biggest debt of gratitude is owed to my wife, Crystal. Her support and helpful suggestions smoothed the entire writing process for me. As always, she patiently gave of her time, even when she had much better things to do like finish chapters for her doctoral thesis. I am the luckiest man in the world to be married to her. It is to Crystal that I dedicate this book.

Glen C. Phillips
London, Ontario, Canada, March 1999

INTRODUCTION

Under the terms of the Municipal Act of 1849, a freshly christened county appeared along the western frontier of Canada West. That county was Lambton, and this book celebrates that achievement. A century and a half ago, Lambton stood as a sparsely settled and comparatively remote region. Authors, travel diarists, and even local residents often referred to it as a backwoods. Indeed, some early chroniclers could be truly unkind, but their nasty descriptions are not really suitable for republishing. However, a combination of nature's bounty, pioneer labours, entrepreneurship, politicking, and, as things turned out, geography transformed Lambton into one of Ontario's most dynamic counties. The following chapters explore the political, economic, and social foundations of the county's heritage. What readers will find is a vibrant and fascinating, although occasionally tragic and violent history.

Admittedly, this book concentrates upon how European peoples shaped the landmass that is now Lambton, and thus it does not address First Nations issues in any great detail. Land claims researchers from Walpole Island, the Sarnia Reserve, and Ottawa have politely informed your author that the First Nations peoples have never been too happy at having those from outside their community portray them in works of history. Indeed, they invariably used the term "misappropriation of their historical voice" to describe the very act of Euro-Canadians writing about First Nations' heritage. So, to ensure that their historical voice does not suffer from misappropriation in subsequent pages, it is thought that such history is best left to those who feel it theirs to write.

At any rate, this book is a picture history and primarily assumes such a format because Victor Lauriston's *Lambton's One Hundred Years: 1849 to 1949* and Jean Elford's, *Canada West's Last Frontier: A History of Lambton*, as fine works in their own right, have made another purely textual approach largely redundant. However, this work is not simply a stand-alone collection of old pictures. While

early images are themselves wonderful historical documents and can tell us an awful lot about the past, the narrative herein presented is historically worthwhile and lends important context to the illustrative material. Essentially, it is intended that these two "halves" go hand in hand and create a whole that is larger than the sum of its parts. Ultimately, it is hoped that readers of all ages will find this format accessible, educational, and, above all, entertaining.

In closing, a word about picture credits is warranted. Sources for the historical images appearing in this book are acknowledged in the credit lines which follow the captions. While many sources have been spelled out in full, space limitations have made the following abbreviations necessary:

AC — *Author's Collection*
LCL — *Lambton Room, Lambton County Library*
LHM — *Lambton Heritage Museum*
JJTRC — *J.J. Talman Regional Collection, University of Western Ontario*
UWO — *University of Western Ontario*

Where possible, the name of the original photographer appears in brackets after the source name. Furthermore, source names in credit lines for multiple images are arranged so that they correspond with images appearing from left to right or, as the case may be, clockwise from the top left. Descriptions in caption titles are organized in a similar fashion.

Finally, it should be noted that the dates which appear in the caption titles refer to when the images were originally created and not necessarily to when the subjects of those images were constructed, born, incorporated, surveyed, etc.

THE EMERGENCE OF A COUNTY

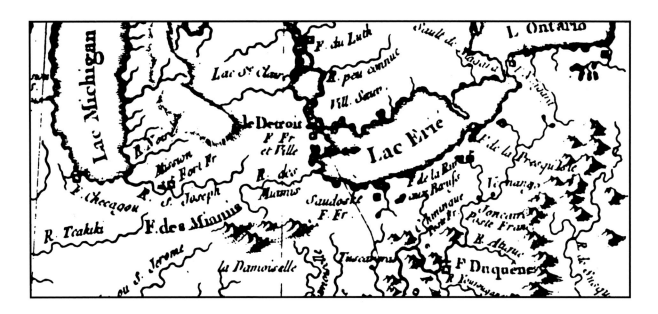

Detail from Bellin's Map of Louisiana, 1764

The French were the first Europeans to explore what is now Lambton County. Although Niagara Falls at first blocked their southerly access to *Lac Huron* and comparatively easy movement along the Ottawa-Mattawa-French river system initially lured them north of the central Great Lakes basin, the French finally pushed their way into the Lambton region during the 1670s. The Sulpician missionaries Dollier and Galinée discovered the St. Clair River (originally Sainte Claire) in 1670, and René-Robert Cavelier de La Salle sailed up the river aboard the *Griffon* in 1679. Thereafter, the French maintained a fairly constant, albeit thin, presence in the area.

As was the custom of the day, the French constructed forts to secure and provision their colony. According to the above map, Fort du Luth stood in the northwest corner of present-day Lambton. However, the actual name and location of this fort are shrouded in mystery. Indeed, Fort du Luth may have been an alternate name for the Fort St. Joseph that the governor of New France ordered the explorer du Luth (also known as Dulhut) to build near the foot of Lake Huron. As to location, Houtan's map of 1689 shows Fort St. Joseph on the site of modern Port Huron, Michigan, and yet later maps put the same fort on the "Canadian" side of the St. Clair. The American historian Burton explained this apparent inconsistency by arguing that this small outpost was originally on the western side of the river, burned down, and was then reconstructed on the eastern side. Still other historians have claimed that the fort was actually at Detroit. Then again, the fort may not have existed at all, as the French were in the habit of sprinkling their maps with ghost forts in order to exaggerate their colonial military strength before the eyes of their chief imperial rivals, the British. *UWO*

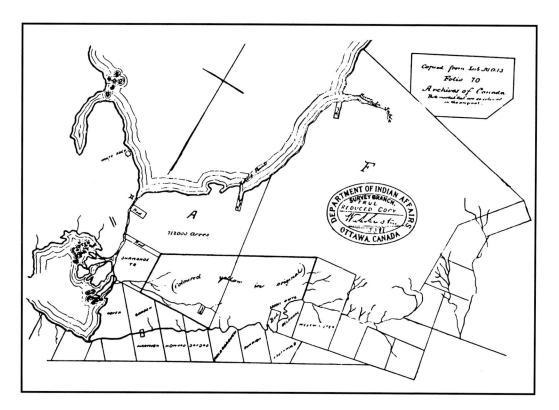

Map of Indian Land Surrenders in Western Upper Canada, circa 1840

Formally ending the Seven Years' War, the Treaty of Paris, signed in 1763, brought New France under the British flag. That same year, King George III issued a proclamation which decreed that the land in and south of the Great Lakes basin was to remain the territory of First Nations peoples in reward for their support of the British during the war. After the American Revolution, the Crown initiated a series of land negotiations with the First Nations protected under the Royal Proclamation of 1763. At first, pockets of land stretching from the banks of the St. Lawrence River to the shores of Lake Erie were needed to compensate the Loyalists who had fought against the victorious American rebels. In later years, the Crown required more land in order to accommodate the flow of immigrants into the burgeoning colony of Upper Canada.

In that part of Upper Canada's Western District which became Lambton, the Chippewas made three land surrenders. Dated September 7, 1796, the first one gave the Crown ownership of the southwest quarter of the county (marked "Shawanoe Tract" on the above map). The southeast quarter passed into Crown possession through the treaty of July 8, 1822 (marked "coloured yellow in original"), and the northern half through the treaty of July 10, 1827 (marked "A"). The last treaty also saw the formation of the Moore, Sarnia, Kettle Point, and Stoney Point Reserves. The Moore Reserve was surrendered on August 18, 1843, and Stoney Point was appropriated by the federal government in 1942 to create Camp Ipperwash. Walpole Island has never been transferred by treaty to the Crown. *UWO*

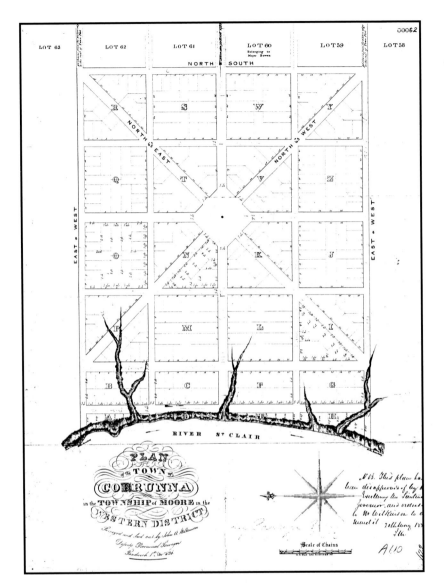

Site Plan of Corunna, 1836

In preparation for the arrival of settlers, the land that the Crown acquired from the Chippewas had to be parcelled into lots demarcated by property lines and road allowances. Aside from commissioning surveys of Lambton's townships, the Upper Canadian government further ordered the establishment of three town plots in the county. Two of these, Warwick and Errol (now half washed into Lake Huron), appeared along the Egremont Road. The third, Corunna, was originally surveyed according to the diagonal pattern depicted to the left. However, this departure from the standard grid layout met official resistance. As the handwritten note on the map's lower right corner reads: "This plan has been disapproved of by His Excellency the Lieutenant Governor, and orders sent to Mr. Wilkinson [the Deputy Provincial Surveyor] are to amend it." And amended it was, as is still shown by the north-south and east-west orientation of the streets in Corunna's core.

Interestingly, Corunna was once considered as a possible site for the capital of the Province of Canada; however, its proximity to the United States readily dashed any hopes in this regard. By the way, note the misspelling of Corunna in the map's title – still a common mistake made today! *Ontario Ministry of Natural Resources*

Head of the St. Clair River at Port Sarnia, from The Penny Magazine for April 29, 1837

Published in London, England by the rather stiffly named Society for the Diffusion of Useful Knowledge, *The Penny Magazine* was but one amongst a legion of journals, newspapers, and published travel diaries that broadcast details about the Upper Canadian frontier to an eager British and Irish audience. While such accounts certainly made for good copy, they also helped to encourage emigration from the British Isles to British North America. After all, the unpleasant prospect of a threadbare existence as a tenant farmer, factory labourer, or nearly insolvent merchant at "home," paled in comparison to idyllic representations of life on the western edge of the Empire. However, many such portrayals revealed less about the realities of Upper Canada and more about the ignorance of their creators. For instance, given the blatant inaccuracies found in the above illustration, including a sun which sets in the south, it is quite likely that the artist had neither visited the St. Clair border region nor experienced the profound hardships which actually welcomed settlers to the raw land. *AC*

"Oaklands," Home of Captain William E. Wright on the Banks of the St. Clair, August 1889

The settlers who at first trickled and then poured into Lambton presented stark contrasts: the young and the old, the strong and the weak, the intelligent and the dull, the honest and the criminal, the dreamers and the embittered, the wealthy and the poor, and so on and so forth. Joining a handful of mostly French-Canadian squatters who had rented land from the Chippewas, these pioneers were primarily Scottish, English, Irish, Canadian, and American.

Notable among the arrivals were retired British naval officers who had served during the Napoleonic Wars. They included Captains A.T.E. Vidal and William E. Wright of Moore Township, Captain George Hyde of Plympton Township, and Captain Richard Emeric Vidal of Port Sarnia. Their appearance in Lambton was largely by official design. Firstly, the British government granted land in the province to veterans as a reward for their military service. Secondly, by settling former military leaders with strong Tory leanings, the Colonial Office and Upper Canada's ruling elite hoped to counter the spread of republican sentiment across the province. To this end, these half-pay officers were appointed as local magistrates, militia commanders, and to other positions of public influence. Even so, the radical reformer William Lyon Mackenzie and his compatriots launched their rebellion in 1837. Upon the uprising's failure, political sympathizers in Lambton assisted some of the fleeing rebels escape to a Yankee refuge. *LCL (E.L. Johnston painting)*

Grace Sutherland, circa 1835

When we think of pioneers, we often think in masculine terms. However, challenging our conventional perspective, the historical record reveals that an approximate average of four females were associated with each male head of household in Lambton County prior to 1862. Indeed, it can be stated unequivocally that women also built the county.

Grace Sutherland, the youngest of five children born to Grace Hogg and Thomas Sutherland, was among the first to settle permanently in Moore Township, doing so in 1833. Like that of all pioneering females, her contribution to establishing her family on the Upper Canadian frontier was significant, if not then publicly acknowledged. In particular, young Grace assisted with household chores, helped out at the family's general store, and otherwise made herself useful. Only her family's relatively privileged position kept her from the more back-breaking tasks, such as wood chopping and farmwork, routinely performed by countless other female settlers in the county. Nevertheless, she did her part according to the domestic expectations of her social class.

In 1847, Grace Sutherland married Dr. Thomas W. Johnston of Port Sarnia. The couple had nine children, seven of whom lived to adulthood. Undoubtedly benefitting from positive maternal guidance, three of Grace's sons rose to local prominence. Thomas, a physician like his father, was a two-term mayor of Sarnia in the late 1890s and sat as West Lambton's member of parliament from 1898 until his death in 1905. Sutherland was a popular Sarnia druggist from 1876 until 1903 and then a well-respected customs officer during the early twentieth century. And Edward served as Sarnia's town clerk for several years until his premature death in 1885. He and his siblings inherited their mother's artistic talents. Edward rendered some of his most interesting, albeit politically cryptic, sketches while jotting down town council minutes. *Hugo Holland*

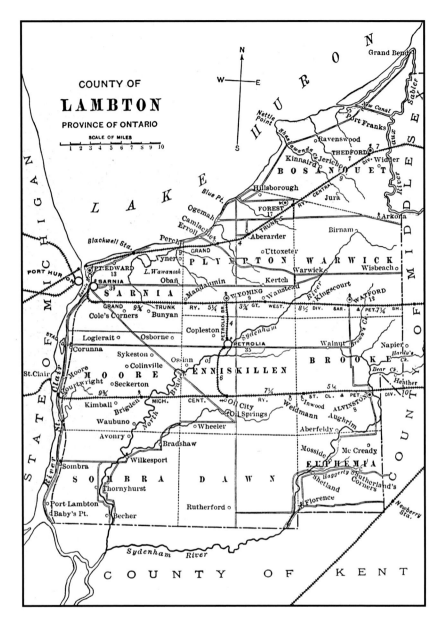

Map of Lambton County, 1885, from the Ontario County Gazetteer

Of Ontario's southern counties, Lambton County was a late bloomer, so to speak. The land mass that became Lambton was initially tucked into the District of Hesse from 1788 until 1791 and then into Kent County of the Western District from 1792 until the middle of the nineteenth century. Although briefly slated to form the District of Moore in 1836, Kent's ten northernmost townships – Bosanquet, Brooke, Dawn, Enniskillen, Euphemia, Moore, Plympton, Sarnia, Sombra, and Warwick – were at last organized into a county of their own by virtue of the Municipal Act of 1849. Named by Malcolm Cameron in commemoration of one of his political heroes (see next page), that county was Lambton.

However, the new county did not immediately enjoy separate municipal status. Rather, since its population did not meet the level legally required for independence, it was united with Essex and Kent. At the beginning of 1851, Kent left this arrangement. Finally, on September 30, 1853, after a year of provisional designation, Lambton was constituted as a fully self-governing county. Port Sarnia (later Sarnia) was selected as the county's municipal seat, and continued as such until Wyoming assumed the position in 1981. When this map was first published, Lambton had made great strides in its development and was a long way from being a nameless appendage to other municipalities. *JJTRC*

John George Lambton, circa 1830

No history of Lambton County is complete without some reference to the English noble "Radical Jack." Born on April 12, 1792 into a family distantly related to the British royals, John George Lambton became Baron Durham in early 1828 and Viscount Lambton and Earl of Durham five years later. His public career, however, betrayed his aristocratic station. As a Whig parliamentarian from 1813 to 1828, and later as a member of Lord Grey's cabinet in the early 1830s, he supported such reform measures as free trade, universal education, Catholic emancipation, dissenters' rights, and electoral reform. At the root of his political sympathies was the belief that since the middle class had contributed enormously to Britain's prosperity, its members deserved a greater share of the nation's political power. To those in the upper class who deemed this concept unconscionable – and they were many – Durham's nickname of "Radical Jack" must have seemed appropriately derisive.

In 1835, he left politics to serve as the British ambassador to Russia. Three years later, Durham became the governor-in-chief of British North America. His official mandate was to sort out the post-rebellion mess in Upper and Lower Canada. Although prematurely resigning the governorship, he still tabled a solution in 1839. Lord Durham's Report proposed the legislative union of Upper and Lower Canada, and urged that the new government's executive branch should be responsible to its elected house. Although not exactly in Durham's suggested forms, union came in 1841 and responsible government in 1848. The Earl died on July 28, 1840. Nine years later, Lambton County was named in his honour. *AC*

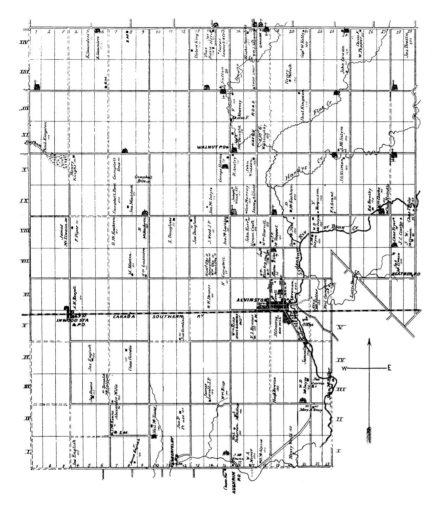

Brooke Township, 1880

The basic unit of administration in nineteenth-century Lambton was the township, of which the county originally contained ten. Laid out and officially opened for settlement over the period 1820-35, local townships were among the last in Upper Canada to be developed. Indeed, of all the townships located in what is now Southwestern Ontario, only the ones in Bruce County and the western half of Grey evolved after Lambton's.

Samuel Smith surveyed Brooke Township in 1832-33. A swamp in the township's western reaches and a thick forest elsewhere curtailed the pace of early settlement. However, by 1861, Brooke's population stood at a respectable 1,600 inhabitants, most of whom were Gaelic-speaking Scottish Highlanders, immigrants from Ireland, and the sons and daughters of United Empire Loyalists who had invoked their land entitlement rights. Named in honour of Lord Brooke, the Earl of Warwick, the township's first municipal meeting occurred on January 3, 1842. Holding a shade over 74,000 acres, Brooke is one of Lambton's largest townships. Subject to approval by the provincial government, the township is set to amalgamate with the Village of Alvinston on January 1, 2001. *AC*

Bosanquet Township, 1880

Lambton's only township to have fallen under the administration of the Canada Company, Bosanquet was named in honour of Charles Bosanquet, the company's inaugural president. The township was laid out in sections over the period 1826 to 1835; however, its first English-speaking settler, Asa Townsend, preceded the first survey party by five years. Perhaps, because the Canada Company initially developed the northern, central, and eastern portions of its Huron Tract (respectively the Goderich, Stratford, and Guelph areas), Bosanquet experienced a slow start. For instance, only 147 settlers resided in the township in 1841. Still, by 1847, enough people had pushed into the area that municipal organization was warranted. Blessed with good soils and some of the county's best natural playgrounds, including Pinery Provincial Park and a string of great beaches, the township was reincorporated into the Town of Bosanquet on December 1, 1994. Along with Forest, Arkona, Grand Bend, and Thedford, Bosanquet is set to form the provisionally named City of North Lambton on January 1, 2001. This will be Lambton's second city. *AC*

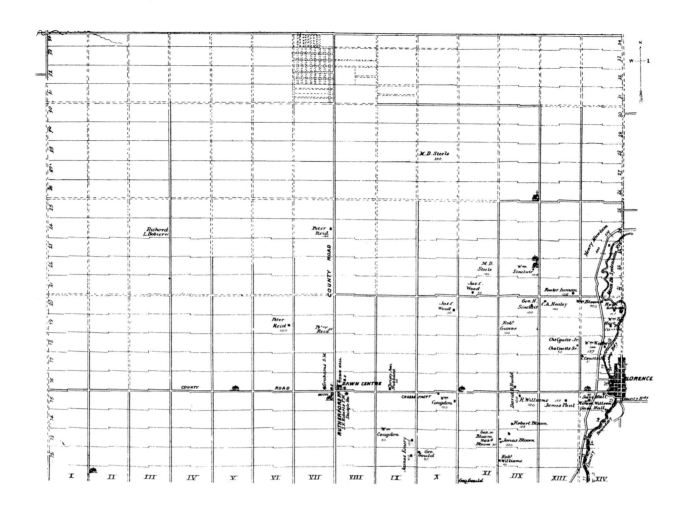

Dawn Township, 1880

One of the earliest townships in Lambton to be developed, Dawn was laid out by Shubal Park in 1821 and originally contained the Gore of Camden (separately constituted twenty-nine years later). Initially, Dawn experienced vigorous growth. By 1846, its 3,320 acres under cultivation were tops in the county. However, poor drainage, particularly in its western half, limited future improvement. By 1880, the township was only one-eighth cleared, making it the least settled area in Lambton. Prior to attaining municipal in-

dependence in 1835, Dawn was joined in varying combinations with townships in Kent. Its appellation stands in contrast to that of its western neighbour, Sombra. As the story goes, when surveyors worked their way out of a thickly forested Sombra, they found themselves bathed in sunlight amid a natural clearing. Struck by the moment, the name Dawn seemed quite appropriate for the new township they were about to map. On January 1, 1998, it united with Euphemia to form the Township of Dawn-Euphemia. *AC*

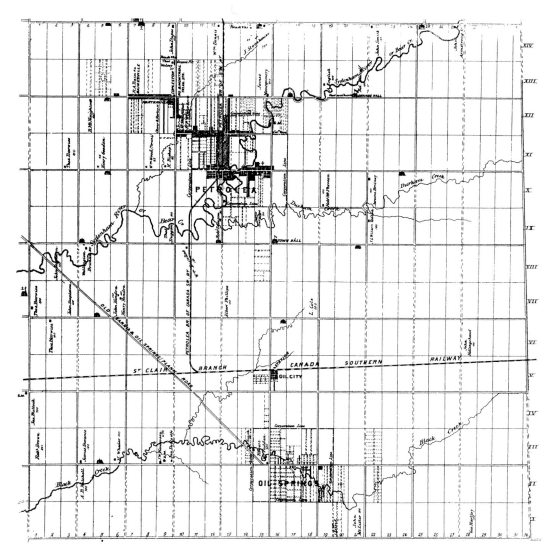

Enniskillen Township, 1880

At just over 82,000 acres, Enniskillen is Lambton's largest township. Named by the Lieutenant-Governor of Upper Canada, Sir John Colborne, in honour of a friend's father, the Earl of Enniskillen, the township was surveyed by Eliakim Malcolm in 1832-33. Dense bush and swamps retarded early settlement. Indeed, Enniskillen was united with Moore in 1850 and then with Brooke from 1851 to 1854 before its government was organized in 1855. Despite a slow beginning, the township was fated to command lasting fame. With the start of the local oil boom in the late 1850s, the name Enniskillen became known throughout the world. *AC*

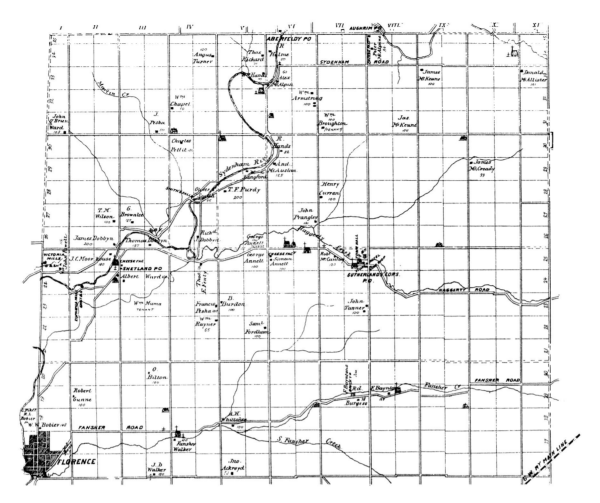

Euphemia Township, 1880

The smallest of Lambton's townships, Euphemia was not created until the Municipal Act of 1849 provided that it be incorporated out of northern Zone Township. However, Euphemia was one of the county's earliest settled and fastest developed townships. Two factors propelled its rapid advancement. One, its early settlement fell under the aegis of Colonel Thomas Talbot, who kept vulturous land speculators at bay, and despite, or perhaps because of his rather irascible and demanding nature, saw that only the most capable settled in the areas under his control. Two, Euphemia's blessing as the best naturally drained region in Lambton was a strong drawing card for pioneers. Upon being surveyed by Samuel Smith in 1822-23, it experienced a sizeable influx of settlers. By 1880, they, their children, and later arrivals had built the township into the county's most prosperous in proportion to its size. Named for the mother of the local M.P.P., Malcolm Cameron, Euphemia amalgamated with its western neighbour, Dawn, on January 1, 1998. *AC*

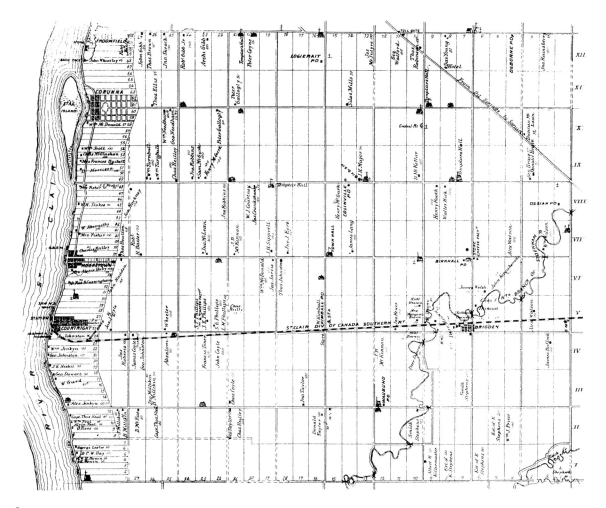

Moore Township, 1880

As was the case in the county's other two riverfront townships, the first whites to settle in Moore were squatters who, beginning around the turn of the eighteenth century, rented land from the local Chippewas. In 1826, the area that later constituted the township joined Sombra Township and Walpole Island to form St. Clair Township. This union lasted until Moore was laid out three years later. While the survey was being completed, Sir John Colborne named it to commemorate his late commander in the Peninsular War, General Sir John Moore. The general had died leading the British against the Spanish during the battle of Corunna in 1809. Organized in 1840, and officially incorporated under the Municipal Act of 1849, the township remained largely rural in character until Chemical Valley reached into it during the 1950s and '60s. After the city of Sarnia, it is currently Lambton's next most industrialized municipality. By virtue of the Sarnia-Lambton Act of 1990, Moore acquired the first concession of the former Sarnia Township. *AC*

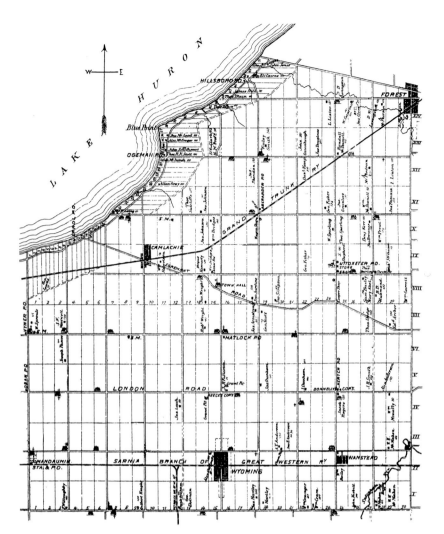

Plympton Township, 1880

Surveyed by Charles Rankin and Peter Carrol over the period 1829-32, Plympton was christened by Sir John Colborne after the town of the same name near Lady Colborne's home in Devonshire, England. Like Dawn, Euphemia, and Warwick, the township also underwent a remarkable early phase of development. Initially settled by British immigrants along the Egremont Road, old countrymen around the Camlachie area, and transplanted Scots from Upper Canada's Lanark County in its southern concessions, Plympton boasted Lambton's second largest township population in 1861 (3,287 souls – only 101 fewer than in Warwick). Moreover, at $841,661 (at least twenty times greater in today's terms), the aggregate value of farms in Plympton was the highest in the county that year. Incorporated on January 1, 1850, the township has generally maintained its rural personality, although its lakefront has become increasingly residential since the early 1970s. If the province gives the nod, Plympton will amalgamate with the Village of Wyoming to form the Town of Plympton-Wyoming on January 1, 2001. *AC*

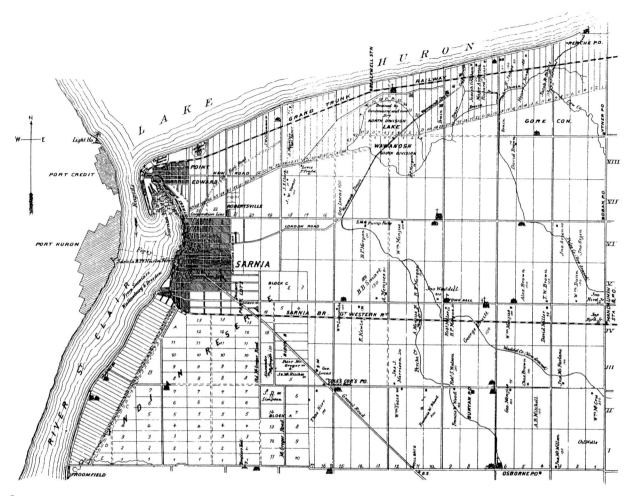

Sarnia Township, 1880

Sarnia Township's first permanent European residents were French squatters who took up land on the banks of the St. Clair during the early nineteenth century. However, the pace of settlement did not pick up until after the local survey was completed over the period 1829-35. Not as selfless this time around, Sir John Colborne named the township after the Roman word for Guernsey, his former home. Municipally organized in 1836, the township is the only one in Lambton to have disappeared. Over the course of the 1800s, small bits of it were nibbled away by its urban neighbour, Sarnia. After the Second World War, Sarnia Township lost even more land to its namesake, with the biggest transfer occurring in 1951, when Sarnia expanded to Murphy Road. In an attempt to stave off later annexation bids, the township reincorporated itself as the Town of Clearwater in 1988. However, on January 1, 1991, the hungry city acquired most of what remained of the former township, and Moore Township annexed its southern concession. *AC*

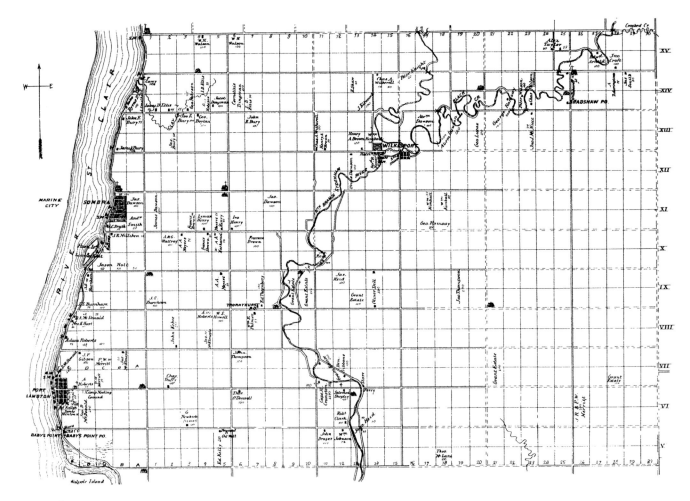

Sombra Township, 1880

Another township initially settled by French squatters during the early nineteenth century, Sombra was surveyed in 1820 and municipally organized two years later. At first, the township was united with Dover to the south, but for three years beginning in 1826, it was united with Moore and Walpole Island to form St. Clair Township. Under the terms of the Municipal Act of 1849 (effective January 1, 1850), Sombra lost its four southern concessions to the newly created Gore of Chatham. Nonetheless, at nearly 72,000 acres, the township remained a substantial one. An economically mixed township today, it supports heavy industry, light manufacturing, a healthy agricultural district, and a notable residential strip along its riverfront. In 1820, Upper Canada's Lieutenant-Governor, Sir Peregrine Maitland, another veteran of the Peninsular War in Spain, named Sombra after the Spanish word for shade. At the time, it was a fitting appellation, since the township was then heavily wooded. *AC*

Warwick Township, 1880

After Peter Carrol's survey of 1832, Warwick was opened for settlement the next year. Notable among those who established themselves in the township during the early 1830s were immigrants who arrived under the sponsorship of Lord Egremont. Mostly taking up land along the road named after the English gentleman, they were joined by retired British army veterans. Indeed, enough people had settled in the township by 1835, that local government was organized that year. Although poor harvests marked Warwick's first several years, within a generation, its residents had transformed their land into some of Lambton's most productive. In 1861, for instance, the aggregate value of farms in the township stood at $803,304 (at least twenty times greater in today's terms). This figure was the second highest recorded in the county that year, and only a slim $38,357 (five percent) behind Plympton's return. Named after the Earl of Warwick, the township amalgamated with the Village of Watford on January 1, 1998. *AC*

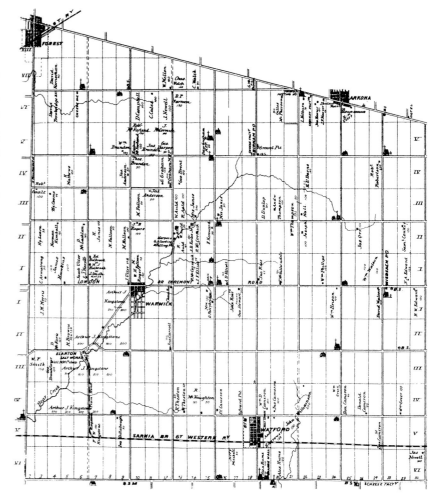

STREETSCAPES

Front Street, Looking South from Lochiel Street, Sarnia, 1869

Although first settled by French squatters during the very early 1800s, Sarnia, or Les Chutes (The Rapids) as it was initially called, did not truly begin to develop until the 1830s. During that decade, the Vidals, George Durand, and, above all, Malcolm Cameron, laid Sarnia's foundations by having a townsite surveyed, establishing local mills and stores, and using their political and commercial influence to their village's benefit (see pages 71 and 99). However, while the competitive spirit of Sarnia's founders fuelled local advancement, it occasionally led to public disputes. For instance, petty feuding underscored the village's renaming. Members of Cameron's faction put forward the name Glasgow to commemorate their Scottish ancestry. The Vidals countered with Buenos Ayres in tribute to their Spanish heritage. Meanwhile, Durand's camp argued that the village should be called after its township. Settling the debate with a vote held on January 4, 1836, a majority of the village's ratepayers chose the latter option, and the place was thus named Port Sarnia. With town incorporation on January 1, 1857, the "Port" was dropped. Sarnia officially achieved city status on May 7, 1914. *AC*

East Side of St. Clair Parkway, Looking South, Courtright, circa 1930
& North Side of Michigan Avenue, Looking West, Point Edward, circa 1920

That great herald of Victorian progress, the railroad, had a profound impact upon Lambton's development. Indeed, the marvel of transportation either gave rise to entirely new municipalities or spurred the advancement of existing communities. Courtright and Point Edward are excellent examples of this phenomena. In the early 1870s, the Canada Southern Railway selected a spot just south of Mooretown for its western terminus. In true nineteenth-century fashion, a swarm of land speculators, commercial entrepreneurs, and industrial developers scooped up property in the area and began to promote their investments. The tracks finally reached the St. Clair River in mid-1873. Ever grateful to the Canada Southern, local residents named their recently born village after Milton Courtright, the railroad's president. Courtright incorporated as a police village in 1901 and as an independent village six years later. In 1975, it gave up this status and officially rejoined Moore Township.

Point Edward's history aptly demonstrates how the arrival of a rail line could trigger remarkable growth in an already established community. Named in tribute to Queen Victoria's father, Edward, the Duke of Kent, but also known as Huron Village until the 1860s, the Point boomed when the Grand Trunk Railway designated the place as the western terminus for its northern branch. To "bridge" the St. Clair, the Grand Trunk constructed a large car ferry facility at Point Edward in the late 1850s. To accommodate ferrying operations, the railroad also laid out a vast rail yard in the village (see page 101). Not surprisingly, Grand Trunk workers poured into the place. In 1866, a directory publisher described the rail centre in one simple word: "flourishing." Point Edward incorporated as a village in 1878. Despite repeated overtures from its rather covetous neighbour, Sarnia, the Point has remained "progressively independent" ever since. *LHM (J.E. Evans photo), LHM*

North Side of James Street, Looking East from Inwood Road, Inwood, circa 1905
& West Side of Brigden Road, Looking North from Boswell Street, Brigden, circa 1900

Inwood and Brigden owe their existence to the interrelationship between the Canada Southern Railway and private entrepreneurs. Beside serving as a travel route across the county's mid-section, the Canada Southern also opened up central Lambton's forests to large-scale commercial exploitation. Seizing the opportunity, the firm of Holmes, Moore and Courtright (the Courtright being a nephew of the railway's president) purchased a parcel of land along the rail line in western Brooke Township and seeded it with a sawmill and stave factory. One of the partners, C.H. Moore, named the new village after Inwood, New York. As per Holmes, Moore and Courtright's moral outlook, lots in the newly established community were sold only to those who pledged not to consume, sell, or manufacture alcoholic drinks. As the *St. Thomas Journal* remarked in May of 1874: "It is thus a teetotal village." Inwood became a police village in 1920 and continued as such until that status was dissolved seventy years later.

At the other end of the county, Nathaniel Boswell recognized the commercial potential that the Canada Southern offered to the eastern part of Moore Township. In 1873, he surveyed and founded Brigden, a village which he named after William Wharton Brigden, a construction engineer in the railway's employ. While Boswell's milling operations gave Brigden its start, a host of other businesses furthered local advancement. Moreover, as a village established in what was once a relatively isolated rural area, Brigden quickly became an important agricultural centre. Existing as an incorporated police village from 1903 until 1975, Brigden still maintains strong links with the farming sector. Its annual fall fair (see page 106) is famous throughout the province. By the way, the rare image to the right was captured about a year before a massive fire destroyed most of the western side of Brigden's main street. Not surprisingly, the devastation encouraged the village's merchants to rebuild in brick. *LHM (Louis Pesha photo), AC (Louis Pesha photo)*

Lyndoch Street, Corunna, circa 1900, St. Clair Parkway, Port Lambton, 1907, & St. Clair Parkway, Sombra, circa 1910

While the Erie and Huron Railway eventually linked and boosted the fortunes of Corunna, Port Lambton, and Sombra, the origins of these communities are rooted in their positions on the St. Clair River. Their first settler-developers, all of whom arrived during the early 1800s, saw the commercial advantages of locating themselves next to the great watery highway. Around their riverfront mills and stores grew the villages that were respectively named after one of the Peninsular War's bloodiest battles, John George Lambton, and the county's southwestern township. Although once incorporated police villages, Corunna, Port Lambton, and Sombra are today joined with their surrounding townships. Interestingly, at just over 6,000 inhabitants, Corunna presently supports the county's second largest urban population. *LCL, LCL, AC (Louis Pesha photo)*

Oil Springs Line, Looking East, Oil Springs, circa 1925
& West Side of Broadway Street, Looking North, Wyoming, circa 1910

As its name suggests, Oil Springs' beginnings are directly tied to the oil industry. Spurred on by the news of James Miller Williams' discovery of oil in the area (see page 81), a tide of romantics, quick-buck artists, and plain, hard-working folks poured into the south-central part of Enniskillen Township in search of their fortunes. Almost over night, a village sprang up where swamp and scrub had previously curtailed development. First known as Black Creek or more formally as the Black Creek Settlement, the new community took on the name of its post office – Oil Springs – on April 1, 1859. Village incorporation came near the end of 1864. Within two years, however, local reserves proved exhaustible, and the frenzied boom came to an abrupt halt. Nevertheless, thanks to Williams' 1858 find, Oil Springs will enjoy everlasting fame as the site of the first commercial oil well in North America.

Initially settled in 1852 by Thomas Brock and then surveyed in 1856 as a stop on the Great Western Railway, Wyoming is another Lambton municipality whose early fortunes were connected to the local oil industry. However, it was less a home to oil production (although it did have a handful of small refineries) and more of an oil transshipment centre. Quite simply, until rail lines reached into Enniskillen, Wyoming was the closest railway point to the oil fields. When incorporated as a village in June 1873, however, Wyoming was moving away from the oil world and becoming more and more of an agricultural centre with mills, specialized shopkeepers, and those in professional practice. Named by Great Western officials after the Pennsylvania town of Wyoming (a word which means "Large Plains" in First Nations), the village is presently the county's seat of government. *LHM, LCL*

Petrolia Line (Petrolia Street), Petrolia, from The Globe *for August 3, 1877*

Petrolia also owes its existence to oil. As drillers spread out from a rather crowded Oil Springs during the very late 1850s, they discovered the black treasure in the vicinity of what was then known as the postal village of Durance. Indeed, they had located enough oil in the area that the name of the Durance post office was appropriately changed to Petrolea on September 30, 1859. Still, Oil Springs managed to maintain its rank as Canada's oil centre for the next several years. However, when the wells began to dry up there, drillers flocked to nearby Petrolea. By the end of 1866, the new focus of the Canadian oil industry had attained incorporated village status. Moreover, Petrolea's pace of growth was so fast that it was proclaimed a town on January 5, 1874. With the achievement of this milestone, the spelling of the municipality's name was officially established as Petrolia.

During the 1870s and 1880s, the oil business was so good that the town surpassed Sarnia in industrial wealth, and the two places challenged each other for bragging rights as Lambton's most populous town. However, Petrolia eventually lost this battle when its fortunes took a temporary turn for the worse around the turn of the nineteenth century (see page 84). Nevertheless, the oil town persevered and, as the county's most enduring boomtown, is presently Lambton's third largest urban centre. *LHM*

Parade along King Street, Looking East from between James & Main Streets, Forest, 1910

A creature of the Grand Trunk Railway and nestled at the convergence of Bosanquet, Plympton, and Warwick Townships, Forest is one of the few communities in Lambton to be named after one of the county's topographical features. During the late 1850s, Grand Trunk train crews nicknamed the place after the dense woods which surrounded the place. The moniker found favour with locals, and when the railway village received its post office on April 1, 1862, the appellation Forest became official.

Benefitting from its central location in north Lambton, Forest quickly outgrew its original role as a Grand Trunk refuelling point. In 1877, five years after the municipality reached incorporated village status, a directory publisher captured the essence of this transformation: "It is one of the most important villages in western Ontario... [and] has progressed so rapidly that it is now a leading centre of trade and manufacture, with a population of 1,300." It should be stressed that the publisher had not simply puffed the place for the sake of boosting sales. According to the industrial census of 1881, the yearly value of goods manufactured in the village stood at $754,600, a figure that bested Sarnia's return by over $215,000! Propelled by a robust and diversified economy, Forest was proclaimed a town in 1888. It will join the provisionally named City of North Lambton on January 1, 2001. *LHM (George A. Hadden photo)*

South Side of Main Street, Looking West, Thedford, circa 1900
& North Side of Main Street, Looking West, Grand Bend, circa 1925

Thedford and Grand Bend, both scheduled to join the City of North Lambton, present an interesting contrast in historical origins. On the one hand, Thedford practically owes its existence to the Grand Trunk Railway, while Grand Bend developed in relative isolation. In the late 1850s, while completing its line from Stratford to Point Edward, the Grand Trunk selected a spot just north of the hamlet of Widder (formerly Pine Hill) as a station site. In 1860, Nelson Southworth gave the railroad some land to support this station, which, despite his desire to have it named Thetford after his hometown in Vermont, was soon called Widder Station. At any rate, the rail connection gave the newly established place a fine beginning. On June 16, 1877, Widder Station was incorporated as the village of Thedford. With incorporation, Southworth at last had his wish answered, albeit in a slightly misspelled fashion.

Removed from the province's railway network and suffering from poor road connections over the first several decades of its existence, Grand Bend developed much more slowly than did Thedford. In 1832, upon receiving a land concession from the Canada Company, Benjamin Brewster and David Smart constructed a saw mill at the hairpin turn of the Ausable River in the northeastern corner of Bosanquet Township. Around this milling operation, destroyed in 1860 by a mob of angry citizens who believed the mill dam was causing their farm fields to flood, clustered a small settlement variously known as Aux Croches, Brewster, Brewster's Mills, or Grand Bend. This last name, taken from the river's course, did not become official until the community received postal designation in 1872. However, the village's somewhat insulated location stunted its advancement until the early twentieth century, when urban vacationers discovered the place as an ideal holiday destination. By the late 1940s, Grand Bend's position as a lakeside resort was firmly entrenched. On June 24, 1951, it finally achieved incorporated village status, a move which saw its northern half in Huron County and its southern half in Lambton County united within the boundary of the latter county. *LHM, LHM (Joseph Senior photo)*

Nauvoo Road, Looking North from the Overpass, Watford, March 13, 1954 & Townsend Line, Looking West from near Richmond Street, Arkona, circa 1925

Watford and Arkona also have contrasting early histories. The younger of the two, Watford was first settled in the early 1850s, but had its fortunes materially boosted when, in 1858, it became the midpoint on the London-Sarnia branch of the Great Western Railway. The village seized the opportunities presented by the railroad. For instance, the editor of an 1866 county directory noted Watford's role in agricultural affairs: "This village is rapidly growing into importance, and is the principal market for the Townships of Warwick and Brooke." Besides giving the place its own hinterland, the railway also allowed it to participate in Canada's expanding industrial economy. During the late 1860s and 1870s, manufacturers located in Watford in order to distribute their processed grains, wood products, and farm machinery throughout the province via the Great Western. Even W.P. McLaren, the local druggist, recognized the commercial advantages offered by the railway. During the last quarter of the nineteenth century, he used its network to ship

his patented inks and writing fluids to customers across Southern Ontario. Incorporated as a village in 1873 and recently amalgamated with Warwick Township, Watford was named in 1854 after Watford, England.

Although Asa Townsend had arrived in the area in 1821, Arkona did not truly get its start until the 1830s, when its townsite was settled and developed. Despite its early foundations and unlike so many other Lambton communities, Arkona never enjoyed having a direct railway link. While this circumstance limited its potential growth, the village nonetheless found respect as a modest, though busy agricultural centre. Village incorporation came in 1876 and will last until the establishment of the provisionally named City of North Lambton on January 1, 2001. Contrary to popular belief, Arkona was not named for Akron, Ohio. Rather, around 1856, it took its name from the Germanic town of Arkona on Rügen, an island in the Baltic Sea. *AC, LHM*

River Street, Looking South from near Centre Street, Alvinston, circa 1950
& West Side of Florence Road, Looking North from near Fansher Road, Florence, circa 1905

The municipal histories of Alvinston and Florence further demonstrate the dichotomous influence of the railroad upon the fortunes of Victorian communities. Initially settled in the 1830s, Alvinston experienced the positive effects of having a railway pass through it. In 1866, six years prior to the arrival of the Canada Southern Railway, a county directory editor did his best to muster the following local description: "The chief business of the place consists of a store, a grist and saw mill, and a hotel." After all, what more could be said about a sleepy hamlet of 100 souls? However, less than a decade after the first Canada Southern train puffed into Alvinston, Lovell's Ontario Directory for 1882 noted that the then bustling centre of 1,000 residents contained "6 churches, a branch bank, 3 saw mills, 2 stave factories, 1 sash, door and planing mill, and 1 flouring mill." Indeed, the railroad could change a place that much and that quickly. A spelling corruption of Alverston on the Isle of Wight, Alvinston was incorporated as a village in 1880.

Founded in the late 1820s, surveyed into lots a few years later, and named in 1856 after either the famous Italian city or the heroic nurse Florence Nightingale (nobody knows for sure), Florence followed a different course of development than did Alvinston. At first, Florence advanced with great gusto. Indeed, during the late 1840s and into the 1850s, it stood as one of Lambton's fastest growing communities. However, as events turned out, this peak was never really surpassed. Significantly, when constructed during the mid-1850s, the Great Western Railway's branch route from London to Windsor bypassed Florence by several miles to the southeast. Thus ignored, the village's hopes of becoming a major centre were thereby dashed. Yet, unlike so many other places in the province that simply shrivelled into ghost towns after not receiving railway blessings, Florence managed to survive. An incorporated police village from 1903 until 1990, it continues to anchor southeast Lambton. *AC, AC (Louis Pesha photo)*

A BY-LAW

For the Preservation of the Public Morals within the Township of Bosanquet.

Passed 5th October, A. D. 1874.

Whereas under the provisions of the Municipal Institutions Act of the Province of Ontario, 36 Vic. cap. 48, power is given to Township Councils to pass By-laws for the preservation of Public Morals :---

Be it therefore enacted by the Township Council of Bosanquet in Council assembled under the authority of the Municipal Institutions Act, 36 Victoria. cap. 48, Sec. 379, Sub-sec. 31.

1. That it shall not be lawful to sell or give intoxicating drink of any sort to any child, apprentice, servant, idiot or insane person, within this Township without the consent of the parent, master, legal protector, or physician of such person or child.

2. That it shall not be lawful for any person to print or circulate any indecent placards, writings, pictures or drawings, on any walls or fences, or any place whatever, or to circulate the same within this Township.

3. That it shall not be lawful for any person or persons to be drunk or guilty of any drunkenness or disorderly conduct, or to utter or employ any profane oath, or any obscene indecent, blasphemous, or grossly insulting language within this Township.

4. That it shall not be lawful for any person to run horses either on horseback or in carriages, or vehicles of any sort on any of the public streets, or highways within this township.

5. That it shall not be lawful for any person indecently to expose his or her person, or be guilty of any indecent, immoral, or scandalous behaviour, or to be found to be wandering about as a common vagrant or mendicant, without any visible means of support, in any street, highway or public place within this Township.

6. And be it further enacted, that any person or persons guilty of a violation of any of the provisions of this By-law, shall upon conviction before any justice or justices of the peace having jurisdiction in the said Township, be liable to a fine of not more than Twenty Dollars, nor less than One Dollar, to be collected by distress and sale of the goods and chattels of the said offender or offenders ; and in case no goods and chattels are found belonging to the said offender or offenders, as aforesaid, on which to levy any fines or fees as aforesaid it shall be lawful for any such Justice or Justices of the peace to commit the offender or offenders to the Common Jail or Lock-up within the County of Lambton, for a period of not more than twenty days, or less than one day as the said Justice or Justices may determine.

7. And be it further enacted, that all fines and penalties imposed and collected under and by virtue of this By-law, shall belong to and be appropriated to the use and benefit of the said Township of Bosanquet.

T. F. EASTMAN,   ROBERT RAE,
          CLERK.   REEVE.

Printed at the " Herald " Office, Thedford.

Public Morals By-Law Broadside, 1874

As is the case today, municipal administration was the level of government which most often touched the daily lives of Canadians during the nineteenth century. Constituted under provincial law, townships, police villages, incorporated villages, towns, cities, and counties were vested, although not entirely, with the responsibility of providing services and regulating the actions of those within their boundaries. In this regard, local councils passed by-laws which dealt with practical or moral issues. Among other things, municipal statutes of a practical nature required that residents clear snow from the walks in front of their homes and keep their poultry, swine, and bovines adequately penned. Meanwhile, by-laws directed at public morality, that oh so prominent of Victorian social themes, are well-represented in this broadside facsimile. Now, lest you poke fun at Bosanqueters for their historical uprightness, remember that every other Lambton municipality passed a similar code of behaviour at one time or another. *LHM*

Petrolia's Fire Department, Central Station, circa 1895

Unlike today, the range of services provided by local governments during the Victorian age was fairly limited, although it usually expanded as communities grew and matured. Road maintenance and drainage constituted the most basic municipal services provided by young and/or small municipalities, such as the county's townships and villages during their formative years. At the other extreme, larger places, such as Forest, Petrolia, and Sarnia, enjoyed consequently larger tax bases and could thus afford sidewalks, police and fire protection, water and sewer systems, street lighting (at first gas, then electric), street paving, markets, public parks, and weekly garbage collection. Besides being a practical necessity, a well-equipped fire department was a point of local pride. Near the end of the nineteenth century, Petrolia boasted Lambton's finest firefighting squad, headquartered in the northeast corner of Victoria Hall. *LHM*

Brooke Township School Section #10, Northwest Corner of La Salle Line & Hardy Creek Road, circa 1925

School administration has long been another form of local government in Lambton. Prior to the establishment of the Christian Reformed private school system in the 1950s, the Lambton County Board of Education in 1969, and the Lambton County Roman Catholic Separate School Board in 1969, a raft of individually constituted public, separate, and private boards of trustees administered schools in school sections (divisions within townships), incorporated municipalities, and grammar (secondary) school districts centred in Watford, Forest, Petrolia, and Sarnia. As is the case today, the chief duties of these trustee boards included building and repairing schools, hiring teachers and custodians, purchasing supplies, and implementing the provincially set curriculum.

With a humble log schoolhouse, Brooke's School Section #10 was established in the northeastern corner of the township in 1858. Twelve years later, the original building was replaced by a frame structure. In 1907, the section's trustees authorized the construction of this brick school. Amidst the province's program of rural school consolidation, S.S.#10 was closed in 1961 and its pupils transferred to the newly constructed Brooke Central School. L to R - bottom: ? McLachlan, ? Demsey, unidentified (note the rather sour face), Melvin Powell, unidentified; middle: unidentified, ? McLachlan, Donelda Powell, Jessie McLachlan, unidentified, unidentified; top: John McLean, Mac McLachlan, Jim Hair, Amy Hair (teacher), Margaret McLachlan, Edith Demsey. *LCL (C.H. Foster photo)*

County Courthouse & Registry Office, Sarnia, 1872

In 1852-53, Alexander Mackenzie, an accomplished stonemason and future prime minister, built Lambton's first courthouse (left) on the southeast corner of Christina and Elgin Streets. Thirteen years later, the county's first free-standing registry office (right) was constructed. Although refurbished after a fire in 1916 and replaced in the early 1960s by the current court and jail buildings further north on Christina Street, the original courthouse was a fine structure of cut-stone with an interior trimmed in oak panelling. It also housed the county council chambers and the county jail. The year that this photograph was taken, a provincial inspector glowingly reported that "every part of the gaol [the Victorian term for jail] and the yards were in excellent order, with the utmost cleanliness prevailing throughout." Over the year ending September 30, 1872, the jail held 158 male and 9 female prisoners. Of these, 119 were first-time offenders, 31 were second-time, 8 were third-time, 9 were habitual criminals, 117 were deemed to be intemperate, and one escaped. Prisoners included 79 Canadian-born, 44 Irish-born, 27 English-born, 11 Scottish-born, and 6 American-born. In addition, at 57 convictions, the most common sentence that year was for drunk and disorderly behaviour. *LCL*

LIST OF CONSTABLES

TILTON HOWARD, High Constable.

TOWNSHIP OF BOSANQUET.—Arkona, P.O.—Uriah Britton, Joel Eastman, Nordale Eastman, William H. Jackson. Widder Station—John Dallas. Widder P.O.—Charles Megg, John Allen, Joseph Truan, John H. Cornell, George Trimbel, Thomas Mason, Alexander Howye, John Mitchell, James D. Morgan. Golden Creek P.O.—William Roy, Jonathan Linsay. Forest P.O.—Calvin Martin, William Bradley, James Bailey, Thomas Martin. Hillsboro' P.O.—Thomas Kindall, Mark Wellington, Thomas Symington, Jr.

TOWNSHIP OF BROOKE.—Watford P.O.—James Slater, William Ellis, Isaiah Saunders, Geo. Finch, William J. Marshall, John Short, Dan'l McAlpine. Aughrim P.O.—Richard Dawson, James Hands.

TOWNSHIP OF ENNISKILLEN.—Ennis P.O.—Robert Montgomery, William Dennis, sen.—Ossian P.O.—David Brichan, Alexander Ingram, jun., Henry Wheeler. Oil Springs P.O.—John T. McKay, George H. Lee, John Savage.

TOWNSHIP OF EUPHEMIA.—Florence P.O.—Richard D. Ackland, James Price, John Scott, William Shepherd, Arthur Bobier, Duncan M. Kerby, Matthew Thompson, Wm. D. Webster. Aughrim P.O.—William Burr.

TOWNSHIP OF DAWN.—John R. Boylan, Solomon Huff, Samuel Hall.

TOWNSHIP OF MOORE.—Corunna P.O.—Hugh McLaren, John Chislett, Peter Lapier, Joseph Simpson. Moore P.O.—David Cronkhite, Joseph Whitsett, John Coulter. Birkhall P.O.—Robert Brown, John Mackenzie. Sarnia P.O.—Isaac Impett.

TOWN OF SARNIA.—William G. Harkness, Samuel Hitchcock, Dyer Howard, Richard Ellison, David W. Finch, James McKelvie, James Stewart, James Holden, William McElheron, James Foulds, Arthur Delmage, Jas. Symington, Alex. Symington.

TOWNSHIP OF SARNIA.—Sarnia P.O.—Daniel Eveland, Abraham Slocum, James Beattie, Thomas Kinsley, Benjamin Slaight, Robert Miller, Thomas Brown, Andrew Hamilton, Walter Wake, William M. Simpson. Mandaumin P.O.—John Bird, jun.

TOWNSHIP OF PLYMPTON.—Kertch P.O.—E. A. Jones. Wyoming P.O.—Wm. Minielly, Samuel P. Fowler. Wanstead P.O.—Archibald Anderson. Oban P.O.—James Carr. Mandaumin P.O.—Thomas Donald. Errol P.O.—Benjamin Schram, Alvah Trusler, William Robertson.

TOWNSHIP OF SOMBRA.—Sombra P.O.—Samuel Hart. Baby's Point P.O.—John D. McDonald, Wm. Dennis Adams, Sidney F. Cook. Wilkesport P.O.—Peter Cullen, Henry Brown, James Robertson, Henry J. Meyers.

TOWNSHIP OF WARWICK.—Warwick P.O.—Chas. Smith, James Bailey, Richard Evans, Maurice Falone, Geo. Smith. Watford P.O.—John Williams. Wisbeach, P.O.—Samuel Howden.

P. T. POUSSETT, C. of P.

Sarnia, April 21, 1863.

Schedule of County Constables for 1863

In Victorian and early twentieth-century Lambton, a network of county constables upheld the law. Aside from generally keeping the peace, these constables enforced federal and provincial statutes, criminal laws, and local by-laws. Of course, accomplishing all of this entailed walking beats, investigating crimes, swearing out warrants against offenders, executing arrest and search warrants, apprehending and locking up suspects, guarding and escorting prisoners to and from court, and testifying at hearings and trials. In essence, their duties presaged those of a modern-day police force.

Appointed annually, county constables drew salaries and received compensation for costs, such as travel fares, they incurred while on the job. However, unlike today's police, they generally wore no official uniform and they usually served part-time, as they worked at other occupations first and foremost. Indeed, the opposite slate of appointees includes farmers, blacksmiths, merchants, hoteliers, and at least one saloon-keeper. The services of Lambton's constables were largely made redundant with the adoption of municipal police forces in Sarnia, Forest, and Petrolia in the late nineteenth century and the formation of the Ontario Provincial Police in 1909-10. Since the OPP's creation, Point Edward, Kettle Point, and Walpole Island have each organized and maintained a local police service. *AC*

Lorne Henderson,
Lambton County Warden, 1957

Born in Enniskillen Township on October 31, 1920, Lorne Charles Henderson was the county's most prominent politician during the second half of the twentieth century. Interestingly, his lengthy public career began almost by accident in 1946, when he successfully ran for Enniskillen Township Council. A man of strong resolve, he had decided to enter the municipal race that year in response to a local councillor who, when criticized by Henderson, retorted: "If you think that you can do a better job, then why don't you run for office yourself?" Henderson held his seat as a township councillor for three more terms. In 1950-51, he served as Enniskillen's deputy reeve and then as its reeve from 1952-57. In his last year as reeve, Henderson, at age 36, became the youngest warden in Lambton County's history.

After a five-year hiatus from politics, during which time he was Enniskillen's municipal assessor, Henderson re-entered the public arena in 1963, when electors sent him to the Ontario legislature as the Conservative member for Lambton East (later Lambton). He served his constituents well and was re-elected five more times. While at Queen's Park, he sat on numerous select committees (chairing some) and occupied the following cabinet positions under Premier Bill Davis: Minister Without Portfolio (1975-78), Minister of Government Services (1978-79), Minister of Agriculture and Food (1979-82), and was then with the Provincial Secretariat for Resources Development (1982-83). In 1983, his request to leave cabinet was granted. Two years later, he retired from politics to be closer to his family and farm in Enniskillen, but has stayed quite active in community organizations ever since. The Lorne C. Henderson Conservation Area just west of Petrolia is named in his honour. *LCL*

CANADIAN Illustrated News

VOL. XI.—No. 6.   MONTREAL, SATURDAY, FEBRUARY 6, 1875.   { SINGLE COPIES, TEN CENTS. } { $4 PER YEAR IN ADVANCE. }

SETTING THE TASK.

SCHOOLMISTRESS, (*Canada*) : There's plenty work for you Aleck ! If you get through those problems, to my satisfaction, in the next three months, you'll remain head of the class, my boy!

Lampooning the Issues Facing Prime Minister Alexander Mackenzie, from the Canadian Illustrated News *for February 6, 1875*

Born on January 28, 1822 in Logierait, Scotland, Alexander Mackenzie is the only Lambton politician to have become prime minister. A stonemason, Mackenzie emigrated to Kingston, Canada West in 1842, but joined his family in Port Sarnia four years later. In the village, he carried on his trade. One of the few authenticated examples of his craftsmanship that still stands is the house which he built for his brother, John, at 316 Christina Street North in Sarnia.

Mackenzie became involved in politics upon arriving in Port Sarnia. His egalitarian views, belief in individual enterprise, and faith in free-market economics saw him gravitate to the Reformers (precursors to the Liberals). In 1861, Lambton's electors sent him to the provincial assembly. After Confederation, his constituents chose him as their federal member. They re-elected him in 1872 and 1874. He also sat provincially for Middlesex West from 1871 until 1872, the year when dual representation ended in Ontario.

In March 1873, the Liberals picked the Sarnian as their leader. Later that year, when Sir John A.'s scandal-ridden government resigned, Mackenzie became prime minister. Anxious to have the stamp of public confidence, he called an election that he and his party won in January 1874. Upon entering his second year as prime minister, Mackenzie was faced by the issues cleverly portrayed in this cartoon. However, his administration would ultimately be known for creating Canada's Supreme Court, implementing the secret ballot, and passing the Canada Temperance Act. Amidst a severe economic recession, his Liberals fell in the 1878 election. Mackenzie, however, retained his seat. Two years later, owing to failing health and waning support within his party, he resigned the Liberal leadership. Having moved to Toronto, "Old Sandy" thenceforth sat in parliament as the member for York East from 1882 until his death on April 17, 1892. He is buried in Sarnia's Lakeview Cemetery. *JJTRC*

Canada Customs Station, Port Lambton, circa 1950 & Post Office, Mooretown, circa 1905

Since the nineteenth-century, customs inspection and postal service have been two of the most prominent federal functions to have affected the daily lives of Lambtonites. Indeed, even before Port Sarnia was made the county's first point of customs collection in 1836, residents were required to pay import/export duties through Chatham or Sandwich (now part of Windsor). During the 1850s and 1860s, communities along the St. Clair River from Point Edward to Port Lambton were designated as customs outports of Sarnia. Of course, just like today, not everyone in the past was pleased about paying taxes on goods imported into the country. For instance, around 1837 or 1838, Captain Richard Emeric Vidal refused to remit Her Majesty's duty on some supplies he had purchased in Detroit. Adamantly holding to his position, Vidal threatened "to blow out the brains" of Port Sarnia's customs inspector. Even more shocking is that the retired navy captain was appointed to the office a few years later!

Officially going into operation on February 6, 1837, the county's first post offices were at Errol in Plympton Township, Moore (an early name for Mooretown), Warwick, and Port Sarnia. Before these openings, Lambtonites received their mail either by horse-carrier from Chatham or by personally journeying to the post office in that town, London, Sandwich, or Detroit. An especially vital link to the outside world in an age before the proliferation of telecommunications, mail service spread throughout the county as its population grew. By 1900-11, a peak of 89 local post offices dotted Lambton's landscape. Most of them, such as the one in Mooretown, operated as adjuncts to general stores. Over the period from 1911 to 1918, an era which saw the implementation of rural mail delivery, the federal government closed 54 post offices in the county. Further closures came in rounds after the First World War. Presently, there are about two dozen post offices and retail postal outlets in Lambton. *AC, LHM (Louis Pesha photo)*

Everyday People, circa 1885

Middle-class life in Victorian Canada assumed a rather rigid outward appearance. According to the social dictates of the era, proper ladies and gentlemen were to carry themselves in a polite, dignified Christian manner, respect authority and their social betters, be charitable to others, and, above all else, never let themselves fall prey to excesses of the flesh, undue passions, and debauching vices. Moreover, as members of Watford's McLeay and Waugh families and Petrolia's Marshall family demonstrate above, elegant deportment, stylish dress, and good grooming were also important to nineteenth-century sensibilities. Ultimately, pressures to be genteel and fashionable boiled down to one issue: the need to broadcast one's social status. L to R (left photo) - Tena McLeay, Margaret McLeay, Emily Waugh (standing), ? Waugh. The Marshalls are unidentified. *LCL (T.B. Taylor photo), LCL*

THANK GOD my wife Susan has left my bed and board without the least cause or provocation, therefore this is to forbid all persons harbouring or trusting her on my account, as I will pay no debts of her contracting.

his
CLARK X MOULTON.
mark.

Dawn, July 23, 1833.

Parlour, Johnston Residence, 167 Victoria Street North, Sarnia, circa 1895 & "Divorce" Announcement, from The Canadian Emigrant *for August 3, 1833*

Not surprisingly, social dictates also shaped nineteenth-century home life. For instance, forces of status-display greatly affected the interior appearance of Victorian houses. Even the rather modest Johnston residence in Sarnia could hardly escape the requirement that a fashionable home contain a parlour appointed with fine furniture, ceiling-to-floor drapes, fancy carpets, wall hangings, and heaps of bric-a-brac. In addition, social pressures demanded that couples live out their marriages in domestic harmony. However, the "divorce" announcement reminds us that not every nineteenth-century household in Lambton followed the expected matrimonial course. Indeed, it would seem that some were quite pleased with spousal departures. While we may never discover the reason for the Moultons' separation, we do know that unofficial divorces like theirs were far more common than our predecessors cared to admit. By the way, Moulton placed his newspaper advertisement not necessarily out of spite, but for legal reasons. *LCL, UWO*

Petrolia's Knights of Pythias at Victoria Hall, August 6, 1890

A century or so ago, social organizations figured prominently in the cultural fabric of the county. At the forefront were fraternal and ethnic lodges, such as the Masons, Independent Order of Foresters, Independent Order of Oddfellows, Canadian Order of Chosen Friends, Knights of Maccabees, Knights of Pythias, Loyal Orange Order, Knights of Columbus, St. Andrew's Society, St. Patrick's Society, and St. George's Society. Besides socially uniting people, many of these associations offered their members life insurance policies and financial aid during times of distress. Other organiza-

tions, among them the Grange and the Patrons of Industry, largely functioned as political and economic lobby groups. Meanwhile, the Brotherhood of Locomotive Engineers and other workers' unions fought for and protected the rights of labour. In addition, a variety of special groups brought people together to pursue common interests. Often having memberships consisting of both genders, these organizations included church and interfaith associations, temperance, horticultural, debating, and dramatic societies, and literary, art, music, and photography clubs. *LHM*

Women's Institute Meeting at the Home of Mrs. F. Kewley, Sarnia Township, 1913

The Women's Institute (WI), founded nationally in 1897, was very prominent in rural Lambton during the first two-thirds of the twentieth century. Organized across the county, WI branches united women socially and provided them with opportunities for intellectual expression. Most notable in this regard are the detailed local history projects which WI chapters published as Tweedsmuir Histories to mark Canada's heritage. Valuable historical works, these histories are especially insightful because they document the past from a female perspective. L to R - sitting on ground: Stuart Kewley, Gordon Kewley, Sylvia Taylor, Helen Cairns, Mrs. S. Carr, Grace Moore, Jean McGregor, Myrtle Griffin, Helen Craig; seated in 2nd row: Mrs. Werden and baby, Mrs. Shepherd, unidentified, unidentified, Mrs. J. Craig, Mrs. T. Leckie, Mrs. T. Taylor, Mrs. S. Kerr (president), Mrs. W. Leckie, Mrs. J. McLennan, Mrs. J. Johnston, Mrs. G. Hardy, Jennie Lamb, Mrs. J. Moore, Mrs. E. Hutchinson, Mrs. W. Beatty, Mrs. J. Hutchinson, Mrs. Steadman; standing & seated in 3rd row: Mrs. D. Murray, unidentified, Tena Gibb, Mabel Sands, Jessie Gibb, Bessie Turnbull, Mrs. J. Mowbray, Mrs. A. Sim with Flora, Mrs. R. Gibb, Mrs. J. Crockard, Mrs. Nesbitt, Mrs. A. Hossie, Mrs. N. Leckie, Mrs. R. Young, Mrs. J. Carr, Mrs. J. Gibb, Mrs. G. Hutchinson, Mrs. B. Duncan, Mrs. G. Tuck; standing in 4th row: Edith Leckie, Edna Milliken, Lottie Kewley, Mrs. P. McAuley, Mrs. L. Harkness, Maud Milliken, Margaret McAuley, Marie McKeown, Hazel McRitchie, Edith Turnbull, Ethel Murray, Emily Fleck, Velma Annet, Irene McRitchie; on porch: Mrs. O. Milliken, Mrs. F. Kewley, Miss Powell (visiting speaker), Roberta Milliken, Mrs. (Rev.) Dodds, Mildred Leckie, Hazel Leckie, Mrs. H. Cole. *LCL (T.A. Cairns photo)*

Marking Dominion Day, Petrolia, July 1, 1904
& Celebrating Queen Victoria's Diamond Jubilee, Wyoming, 1897

Around the turn of the nineteenth century, Canadian nationalism drew upon Canada's bonds with Great Britain and the confidence Canadians placed in their new country. Indeed, if you were to ask a typical Canadian from the late 1890s who was the leader of the young Dominion, you would likely receive as your answer, "Prime Minister Wilfrid Laurier and Queen Victoria!" As the above images demonstrate, this dual spirit clearly marked Lambton County a hundred years ago. *LCL, LCL*

Funeral Carriages, Front Street, Sarnia, circa 1910

Death is an unescapable fact of life. In contrast to our rather clinical approach to the subject, Victorians and Edwardians confronted the issue in a more open manner. They did so because death took greater prominence in their lives, since people generally died younger and child mortality rates were much higher in their day.

To overcome their grief, our ancestors often undertook a curiously public ritual. First of all, the family of the deceased had memorial cards, usually bordered with thick black lines, circulated to friends and family. According to custom, recipients lovingly preserved these cards in family photograph albums or scrapbooks. At wakes, visitations, and funerals, the dearly departed was often on view in an open coffin. In a similar vein, caskets could also have viewing windows built right into them. Even more macabre to our modern-day sensibilities, photographs of the dead body were sometimes given away as an added gesture of remembrance. Funeral processions were also quite public in that coffins were generally displayed in open-air or, as the above scene illustrates, glass-encased hearses. Family, friends, acquaintances, and, upon the death of a politician or celebrity, public officials accompanied the body to the cemetery. *AC*

Hamming It Up for the Camera, Oil Springs, 1902

If the end of the 1800s is any indication, nothing gives rise to a renewed feeling of confidence than the turn of a century. Perhaps, simply surviving time does the trick. Of course, at the beginning of the twentieth century, Lambton residents had much more concrete things to which they could look. First and foremost, the local and national economies were, by and large, booming. Moreover, "modern" conveniences in the shape of electricity, mechanization, and the automobile were making life increasingly easier. And last but not least, general economic advancement, social progress, and technological developments had combined to give rise to an age with more and more leisure time. In striking contrast to the county's pioneers, a Lambtonite from around 1900 generally clocked a shorter workday, enjoyed a greater relative income, and could choose from a wider range of entertainments. This jovial group of young men certainly captured the spirit of the times before a studio camera in Oil Springs. L to R - bottom: unidentified, Bill Laycock, Bill Moore, Fred Lillywhite, Charles Collins, possibly Ham Laycock; middle: unidentified, Bill Gibson, unidentified; top: unidentified, unidentified. *LCL (Tiderington Brothers photo)*

> # SARNIA BREWERY!
>
> ---◆---
>
> ## GEORGE RUSSELL,
>
> ## MALTSTER & BREWER OF ALE & PORTER,
>
> ### DEALER IN MALT & HOPS.
>
> ~~~~~~~~~
>
> ## FRONT ST., SARNIA, C.W.
>
> In rear of the Bank of Upper Canada.

Directory Advertisement for the Sarnia Brewery, 1864

Lambton, unlike many other counties in Ontario, never fostered a prolific alcohol manufacturing industry during the 1800s. Such was the case because the abstemious nature of many settlers limited the potential market for hard drink and because competition from outside the county kept local distilling and brewing efforts in check. Even so, Florence had a small distillery during the early 1830s and Alvinston had one during the mid-1850s. And in the early to mid-1860s, modest breweries could be found in Moore, Sarnia, and Warwick Townships.

George Russell established the Sarnia Brewery near the St. Clair River (301 North Front Street) in 1861. Despite the steady influx of beer from London, Toronto, and Montreal, his ales and porters proved sufficiently popular with locals that he enjoyed fifteen successful years in business. Indeed, Russell used some of his profits to dabble in real estate along the street in Sarnia which today bears his surname. In 1876, however, failing health forced George to lease the brewery to his brother, John. Illness also struck John, and, unable to find a successor, he abandoned the business altogether. In 1883, A.E. Sinclair leased the brewery, but the subsequent arrival of local-option prohibition plunged him into insolvency. Six years later, the Heuser family from Marine City, Michigan bought the brewery. By then, the dramatically weakened business could hardly challenge more distant brewers for dominance in the Lambton market. Still, the Heusers managed to carry on brewing in the old Russell building until the late 1890s and at another location near Imperial Oil into the very early twentieth century. *AC*

The Alexander House, circa 1885, Peter D. McCallum, 1893 & the Hamilton Hotel, circa 1908

Licensed hotels were the most prominent public drinking places in the county during the nineteenth and early twentieth centuries. In their bars, patrons could enjoy a shot or two of Canada's finest rye whisky, a glass of Pelee Island wine, a tankard of locally brewed ale, or, if the occasion called for something a little less strong, a bottle of soda water or ginger pop. However, Lambton's inns were far more than just watering holes. Above all, they provided lodgings and meals to travellers. Moreover, they assumed important social roles. For instance, barroom customers often exchanged news and business gossip over drinks. More formally, the comparatively large public rooms within hotels functioned as *de facto* community centres when and where other facilities did not exist. In this regard, hotels provided space for banquets, lodge meetings, and, particularly before the mid-nineteenth century, municipal council meetings, school board meetings, and even division court sessions.

Sarnia's Alexander House and Wilkesport's Hamilton Hotel were typical of the hostels which once dotted Lambton County. Although still serving the vital functions described above, rural hotels like John Hamilton's tended to be relatively modest in size. Meanwhile, the urban business climate gave rise to much larger establishments, such as the Alexander House, which, as an interesting sidebar, once served drinks to a visiting Prime Minister John A. Macdonald in 1872. Regardless of location, however, local hotels were subject to federal, provincial, and municipal regulations. Chiefly enforcing these codes were liquor license inspectors, including Peter D. McCallum, who occupied the office for East Lambton from 1906 until 1916. Of all offences, McCallum and his colleague in West Lambton most frequently caught hotelkeepers selling drink during prohibited hours on Sundays and after statutory closing times Mondays through Saturdays. *LCL (J.S. Thom photo), LCL, LCL*

Moral & Physical Thermometer, from the Canada Temperance Advocate *for July 15, 1850*

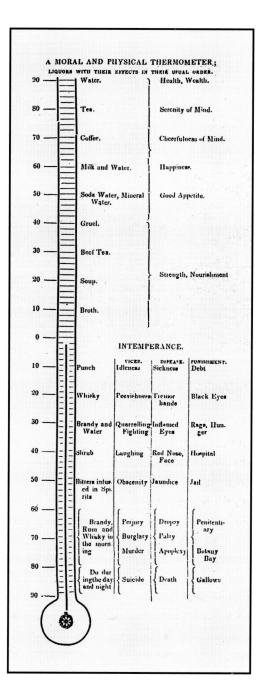

During the late 1700s and early 1800s, a great religious revival struck the English-speaking world. At its heart lay the belief that Christ would return only after all sin had been purged from the globe. The revival particularly swept up Baptists, Presbyterians, and Methodists, who fervently crusaded against a wide array of evils, ranging from blasphemy to drunkenness. By the mid-1820s, the battle against insobriety had coalesced into the temperance movement. Upper Canada's first temperance society was organized in the rather incongruously named Bastard Township (near Brockville) in 1828. Within five years, the reform impulse had reached Lambton County, where it found warm support. Early local hotbeds of temperance sympathy were the Townships of Moore, Plympton, Sarnia, Sombra, and Warwick, as well as Port Sarnia.

At first, the temperance movement literally expected its followers to temper their drinking habits. Personal consumption of liquor was forbidden, although the moderate use of beer, wine, and cider was allowed. Then, during the 1830s and 1840s, temperance societies, fearful of backsliding, gradually adopted teetotal (total abstinence) principles. During the teetotal era, the abstemious increasingly demanded that the rest of society also give up strong drink. To this end, teetotallers, in keeping with their evangelical bearings, used journals, pamphlets, books, and illustrations, including the diagram to the right, to implore their neighbours to stop drinking. However, the wider public refused to bend voluntarily under this pressure. In response, teetotallers next turned to legal means to forward their agenda, and thus began the great prohibition campaign of the Victorian century. Lambtonites assumed national prominence during this phase of the temperance crusade. By the way, how do your vices and virtues rate according to the Thermometer? *JJTRC*

Malcolm Cameron, 1853, Alexander Vidal, circa 1900 & Warren T. Henry, circa 1880

Malcolm Cameron, the Clear Grit politician and founder of Sarnia, stands as Lambton's most prominent early temperance crusader. Locally, he was primarily responsible for forming the Port Sarnia Temperance Society, as well as similar organizations throughout the Western District. However, Cameron devoted his greatest energies to the wider temperance cause. He either chaired or sat on several government select committees that examined the issues of temperance reform and prohibition. More significantly, during the fall of 1852, he tabled the first prohibitory law in the history of the provincial legislature. However, the liquor trade's lobbying saw to the bill's defeat. The Sarnian also held a handful of national temperance offices, including Grand Worthy Patriarch of the Sons of Temperance, Most Worshipful Grand Chief of the Good Templars, and vice-president of the Ontario Prohibitory League.

Senator Alexander Vidal of Sarnia was another notable local apostle of temperance. Most prominently, he sat as the president of the Dominion Alliance for the Total Suppression of the Liquor Traffic from its inception in 1876 until his death in 1906. Formidable in name and in action, the Alliance co-ordinated the prohibition campaign across Canada. The Alliance's greatest Victorian triumph was the passage of the Canada Temperance Act, a statute which the senator from Sarnia had helped to draft and steer through the senate. Vidal's eminent position in the Canadian temperance movement also saw him internationally recognized. For instance, in 1880, the United Kingdom Alliance had him lecture before its membership. The invitation to Vidal represents a rare nineteenth-century example of the Mother Country desiring to learn from the experiences of one of its imperial offspring.

Of course, not every dry advocate in Lambton sought the national stage. Warren T. Henry, for example, played a leading role in temperance matters in Sombra Township. Henry organized local divisions of the Sons of Temperance, chaired temperance meetings, and, most significantly, he energetically campaigned to carry the local-option Canada Temperance Act in his township. In many respects, Henry's contributions to the temperance movement were just as important as Cameron's or Vidal's. After all, the national prohibition agenda would have come to naught without grassroots organizers like him. *AC, LCL (J.S. Thom photo), Laura Babcock*

Cartoon about the Charles Hand Dynamiting, from the Grip for October 9, 1886

The Canada Temperance Act or Scott Act, as it was popularly called after its parliamentary sponsor, inflamed passions on both sides of the prohibition debate. Enacted in 1878 by the government of Lambtonite Prime Minister Alexander Mackenzie, the local-option statute worked at the city or county level and could only come into effect after electors voted to adopt it during a municipal plebiscite.

Lambton's only Scott Act regime began on May 1, 1886 and lasted three years. Local hotelkeepers hardly welcomed the arrival of prohibition. After all, barroom sales constituted a significant part of their revenues. Worsening matters for the trade, on June 9, 1886, the Lambton Scott Act Association, led by J.G. McCrae, successfully petitioned county council to appoint a special police magistrate to preside over Scott Act cases. This appointment was key to the Association's enforcement strategy, and by having M.S. Campbell, a Watford prohibitionist, fill the office, it was hoped that the rather low conviction rates registered in other counties would not happen in Lambton. Not surprisingly, such a swaying of the criminal justice system was intolerable to local hoteliers. On the early morning of June 10, one of their ranks, Sarnian Charles Hand, had J.G. McCrae's residence dynamited in a gesture of intimidation and retaliation.

While the explosion injured no one and caused only minor damage, the Ontario government ordered an undercover police investigation that eventually resulted in the arrest and trial of Hand. However, a sympathetic jury found the hotelkeeper not guilty. The entire affair garnered international press coverage. Amid the sensationalism, J.W. Bengough drew and published this cartoon as an apology to Oliver Mowat, Ontario's Attorney-General (pictured wrestling the bomber's hand or the bomber Hand, if you prefer). Bengough had earlier rebuked Mowat for not investigating previous anti-Scott Act dynamitings in the province. AC

Vol. XXVII.   TORONTO, OCTOBER 9th, 1886.   No. 14.

EDITED BY J.W. BENGOUGH

THE ARRESTED HAND.

ATTORNEY-GENERAL MOWAT'S REPLY TO THE CHESTNUTTY QUESTION—
"WHERE ARE THE POLICE?"

PRICE 5 CENTS PER COPY, $2 PER YEAR.

PUBLISHED EVERY SATURDAY,

By the GRIP PRINTING AND PUBLISHING CO. 26 and 28 Front St. West, Toronto.

Which One?

The Government Protects our orchards from the Cotton-tail rabbit. It protects our vineyards from the San Jose scale. It protects our swine from the hog cholera.

Why not protect the boys from the saloon?

The saloon gets one boy out of every six. Continue to license it, and it will get one of us sure. Which one will you sacrifice?

VOTE FOR LOCAL OPTION AND PROTECT THE BOYS

Prohibition Poster, 1913

From the temperance perspective, Canada's experiment with the Scott Act proved to be a dismal failure. In Ontario, for instance, only a couple dozen municipalities ever adopted the local-option law, and by the late 1880s, they had all repealed it. Nevertheless, the drys regrouped and pushed for all-out prohibition. In 1898, the issue was voted upon across Canada. With a spread of 278,380 ballots for prohibition to 264,693 against, it seemed that the national plebiscite would at last secure a Dominion-wide ban on the sale of beverage alcohol. Lambton's electors pledged their support for prohibition by a margin of 4,107 votes to 1,741. However, Prime Minister Wilfrid Laurier avoided the thorny issue by arguing that his administration could not possibly pass a prohibitory statute because only a quarter of the entire Canadian electorate had participated in the plebiscite.

Thus stymied, the temperance camp again regrouped and launched a renewed campaign for local-option prohibition. To this end, Lambton County's prohibitionists contributed this poster to the national effort to win sympathy for the cause. Presenting a rather emotional, yet persuasive argument, it features a photograph of six young lads from Petrolia. Three years after the poster was first published, drys in Lambton and across the province had their wishes answered with the establishment of provincial prohibition under the Ontario Temperance Act of 1916. L to R - Clare Collins, A. Drope, Kenneth Ferguson, ? McDougall, Wesley Brown, Tom Scarsbrook. *LHM*

Seized Boatload of Smuggled Liquor, Marine City, Michigan, circa 1925

While prohibition under the Ontario Temperance Act from 1916 to 1927 and under various federal statutes, regulations, and orders-in-council in force over the same period fostered domestic boot-legging, the rum running of the era was a response to the American experiment with nation-wide prohibition from 1920 to 1933. Seizing upon the fact that Canadian prohibition – either federal or provincial – only forbade the sale of alcoholic beverages, while U.S. prohibition outlawed their sale *and* manufacture, "exporters" funnelled legally produced Canadian booze through a rather porous border to parched American customers.

With miles and miles of riverbank and lakeshore stretching from Walpole Island to Grand Bend, Lambton served as an ideal staging-ground for smuggling the likes of Corby, Seagram, Walker, Wiser, Labatt, and Carling into the dry Republic. High-powered motor-boats were the preferred conveyance, although boxcars with hidden cargoes of liquor occasionally slipped through the St. Clair Tunnel. Indeed, the "export" business was so lucrative that Casimir Kocot established a brewery and a distillery on Sarnia's waterfront. That his product labels closely resembled those of American brands speaks volumes about his intended market. Of course, as the above scene attests, not every clandestine load of "the precious" evaded the U.S. border patrol. *Gene Buell*

AGRICULTURE

Pioneer Farming on the St. Clair Frontier, circa 1840

In sharp contrast to the rustic images of Upper Canada painted by the print media, a back-breaking greeting to the frontier baptized settlers. Indeed, cutting a life out of the wilds of Lambton County was not for the faint of heart. Upon obtaining land, the newly-arrived had to construct a shelter (often a crude log shack or cabin at first), clear trees, drain the soil, and plant a crop in time for the growing season. Relying upon the good graces of nature for a bountiful and profitable harvest, the county's nineteenth-century farmers lived a precarious existence. After all, storms, droughts, cold spells, ravaging pests, and wholesale damage caused by fungi or rot could easily waste away a year's investment and labour in an age before crop insurance. Still, many persevered and transformed the forests and swamps of Lambton into some of the province's most productive farmland. In doing so, they also laid the county's economic foundation. *LCL*

Making Maple Syrup, Moore Township, circa 1925

While Lambton's forests impeded settlers' efforts to establish farms, the very same trees also played important economic roles in pioneer life. Most obviously, the forest was a vital source of building materials. Trees also offered farmers several commodities to use domestically, sell, or barter. Cordwood, potash from burnt logs, and tree bark with a high tannic acid content, such as that from oak, were respectively used to heat homes, make household soap, and tan animal hides. Moreover, these products found ready demand in the marketplace. For example, storekeepers along the St. Clair River traded for or bought immense quantities of cordwood to resell as steamboat fuel, and commercial agents purchased potash and bark by the barrelful to supply industrial soap and leather manufacturers across the country.

Of course, for those farmers lucky enough to own a stand of the right tree species, the forest was also a source of sugar. Early every spring, the sap of sugar maples was tapped and boiled down into syrup and sugary crystals. According to agricultural census data, Lambton produced 136,946 pounds of maple sugar in 1861. In 1921, the value of maple syrup products made in the county was $24,545. Now, this may not sound like much today, but consider that the average industrial wage that year was around $2 per day. Aside from its commercial sale, maple syrup made its producers money in another major way. Quite simply, the homemade sweetener could be substituted for store-bought refined sugarcane or molasses. *LHM*

Harvesting Hemp on the Fraleigh Farm, Bosanquet Township, circa 1930

The county's first farmers chiefly grew wheat because that grain gave them immediate access to local and well-established regional, national, and international markets. However, the commodity did have its drawbacks, including periodic serious drops in its world price and its susceptibility to the cold and a variety of parasites. In response to these difficulties and in reaction to the development of markets for other crops, such as the demand of area breweries for barley, Lambton farmers diversified their production over the last half of the nineteenth century. Agricultural census figures show that the county's five most significant crops and their corresponding yields in 1851 were wheat (279,989 bushels), corn (182,176 bushels), oats (79,955 bushels), potatoes (55,954 bushels), and peas (26,079 bushels). Census returns fifty years later, besides showing spectacular leaps in production, reveal wheat's relative slide from absolute dominance. In 1901, the five most significant crops and their yields were oats (2,706,790 bushels), wheat (1,051,880 bushels), corn (992,574 bushels), barley (445,799 bushels), and potatoes (365,988 bushels).

The twentieth century witnessed even more interesting crop diversification. For instance, around 1925, Howard Fraleigh began to grow hemp on his farm near Forest. To augment his flax milling business, Fraleigh cultivated hemp as another source of fibre for making binder twine and cordage. However, in 1938, during what Fraleigh's son, Sid Sr., later described as an era tinged with paranoia about the plant, an amendment to the federal Opium and Narcotic Drug Act practically outlawed hemp cultivation, including that done on the Fraleigh farm. The great fear was that the plant could be used for less legitimate purposes. *LHM*

Dairy Cattle Drinking the Waters of the St. Clair River, Courtright, 1909

Animals have been on Lambton farms since the beginning of settlement. At the very least, early farmers usually kept a pig or two and perhaps some poultry as sources of food. If they were lucky, they also had a cow or a couple of goats to provide milk, some hens for eggs, and a few sheep for wool. Horses, donkeys, mules, oxen, cattle, and sometimes even dogs, were used as forms of motive power. However, during the latter half of the nineteenth century, growing markets for animal products, along with increasingly improved access to these markets, encouraged many county farmers to move into

raising stock. This phase of diversification followed two courses: dairying, a response to a rapidly expanding Canadian cheesemaking industry, and stock-breeding, a response to the rise of the trans-Atlantic meat-packing business. Participation in these export-driven industries drew Lambton's agriculturalists into yet other international economies. Over the course of 1882, for example, farmers in north Lambton shipped to Britain via the Forest Grand Trunk Railway station over 4,000 head of beef cattle and about 7,000 sheep and lambs. *AC (Louis Pesha photo)*

Threshing on the Weaver Farm, Lot 6, Concession 7, Warwick Township, circa 1900 & Haying on James, George & John Skinner's Farm, Lot 14, Concession 6, Dawn Township, 1918

Just as is the case today, the most important phase of the agricultural season was the harvest. After all, this was the time of the year when the farm family's labour yielded a return or proved for naught. These photographs present an interesting contrast in harvesting methods in Lambton's past and speak to the economic issues that informed the adoption of such methods.

Given the price fluctuations in commodity markets, timing exactly when to take cash crops off the field crucially affected the bottom line. This timing requirement, along with growing field acreages and the dictates of climate, encouraged farmers to adopt mechanized grain harvesting techniques. Thus, over the course of the nineteenth century and into the twentieth, the use of steam-powered threshing machines, such as the one owned by Thomas and William Venning pictured above, became more and more prevalent in the county. Although purchasing or hiring a threshing outfit required money, the increased and immediate yields which resulted outweighed the extra costs involved.

On the other hand, hay, generally not subject to the same market forces as cash crops, did not usually call for rapid harvesting and could thus be gathered manually. This is not to imply that the Skinners were behind the times. Instead, they merely chose to substitute their own labour for the cost of mechanical haying. Such sensible applications of economics are still important farming skills practised in Lambton today. *LHM, LCL*

Barn Raising on the John Marsh Farm, 1920 Moore Line, Moore Township, 1897

As the county's agricultural sector matured, small outbuildings on farms generally became unsuited to their original functions. Consequently, during the late 1800s and early 1900s, they were replaced by barns sufficiently spacious to house livestock, feed, harvested grain, and machinery under one roof. Framed with skeletons of heavy wooden beams and underpinned by cement-block or poured concrete foundation walls, these barns symbolize two prominent features of farm life. One, since they required a mass of people to construct them, such as this group gathered at John Marsh's barn-raising bee, they represent the strong social bonds that characterized Lambton's rural community. Two, they also illustrate the march of agricultural progress a century ago. Indeed, given that many of these barns still stand today (including this one), they are living testaments to our ancestors' accomplishments. *Moore Museum*

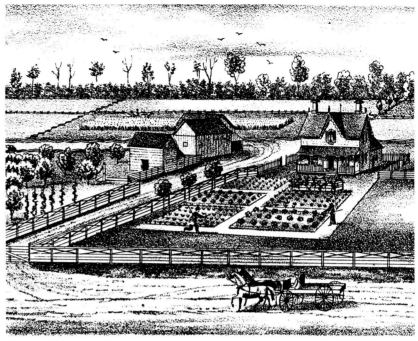

W. Auld Residence (above left), 1880, J. Hartley Residence (above right), 1880 & T. Graham Residence (left), circa 1905

Another prominent symbol of agricultural progress in nineteenth-century Lambton was the fashionable rural residence. Within a generation or two of initial settlement, many local farm families could afford to replace old log cabins and simple frame dwellings with substantial homes like these classic interpretations of Ontario Gothic Revival architecture. In this regard, farmers were no different from their urban cousins, as they sought to display their affluence and status in brick and stone. These houses are still standing as the Geerts' home, 6510 First School Road, Warwick Twp. (Auld residence); the Korvemakers' home, 5067 Minielly Road, Plympton Twp. (Hartley residence); and the Elliotts' home, 6784 Bentpath Line, Dawn-Euphemia Twp. (Graham residence). *AC, AC, LCL*

COMMERCE

TONTINE DRUG STORE!

MRS. ADAMSON,

DEALER IN

DRUGS, MEDICINES, PERFUMERY,

SCHOOL BOOKS, STATIONERY, FANCY GOODS, &c.,

MAIN STREET, OIL SPRINGS.

Prescriptions carefully compounded.

*Directory Advertisement for the Tontine Drug Store,
Oil Springs, 1866 & Elizabeth Adamson, Oil Springs, circa 1888*

As late as the 1960s, women owned a relatively small percentage of the retail trade in Lambton. However, female pioneers can be found in the county's business past. Refusing to bend before the social traditions and legal-commercial customs of her era, Elizabeth Adamson stands as, perhaps, the most prominent example in this regard. Settling at Oil Springs in 1863, she at first worked as an assistant in the drug store of Dr. Samuel Macklem. Under his direction, Adamson studied the art and science of pharmacy. In 1866, she purchased the doctor's stock of herbs, chemicals, and medicines and struck out on her own. Not long afterwards, Adamson became the province's first licensed female pharmacist. After the collapse of the local oil boom, most retailers in Oil Springs either plunged into insolvency or abandoned the village altogether. The druggist persevered. However, to keep her shop afloat, she wisely diversified her stock to include a line of groceries. Adamson stayed in business until she was in her late fifties. In 1886, her daughter, Lucy, assumed the store's management. A few years later, John Windlow bought the pharmacy. *LHM, Oil Museum of Canada*

J.T. Locke's "The Ark," Corunna (above),
G.M. Shepardson's General Store, Sombra (opposite top)
& J. Brewer's General Store, Sunnyside (opposite bottom), all circa 1905

From the time when Lambton was opened for settlement until they started to disappear in great numbers beginning in the 1920s, general stores, scattered across the rural and urban landscape, were the county's most common variety of retail business. Within their walls, one could find for sale everything from foodstuffs to patent medicines to clothing to kitchen sinks. However, aside from their obvious commercial functions, general stores also played significant social roles in their communities. Most notably, their proprietors actively encouraged locals to gather at their premises and sit and chat about politics, neighbourhood gossip, and farm business. Of course, storekeepers did not do this merely for reasons of sociability. Indeed, these savvy merchants knew that the longer people spent surrounded by stacks of enticing merchandise and display cases filled with select goods, the more likely those people were to make purchases. *AC, LHM (Louis Pesha photo), LHM (Louis Pesha photo)*

Everest's Cough Syrup.

THIS celebrated Cough Syrup has now been in use for over eight years, and the demand is increasing rapidly every year. Thousands can now testify to its wonderful medicinal power to allay and cure Coughs, Colds, &c. Testimonials are coming in almost daily from all parts of the country of its wonderful curative properties. It is easy and pleasant to take. Children and delicate females can take it with ease and without any danger. Public speakers are now using it to take away that irritating hoarseness caused by long continuous speaking. ☞ ONLY 25C. A BOTTLE. For sale by all dealers.

EVEREST'S LIVER REGULATOR.

THIS Liver Regulator and Blood Purifier acts on the Kidneys, Blood, Liver and Bowels, and is decidedly the best of its kind in the market to-day, of which hundreds can and have testified. A one dollar bottle has been known by many to increase the weight of weakly and delicate persons ten pounds. Write to the undersigned for testimonials as to its virtues. For sale by all dealers.

GEO. M. EVEREST,
MANUFACTURING CHEMIST,
FOREST, ONT.

Back & Front of a Victorian Trade Card, circa 1885

In an age before radio, television, and websites, merchants had to rely on print advertising. Besides placing announcements in local newspapers and county directories, retailers made use of trade cards, which they freely circulated throughout their communities in hopes of drumming up business. Because these marketing novelties were often quite colourful and depicted a wide variety of stock and custom images, they were highly collectible, especially in the Victorian era.

Usually pasted into scrapbooks, they were thus a less ephemeral form of advertising. The above trade card puffed the healing powers of the nostrums manufactured by George M. Everest, a licensed pharmacist who ran two drug stores in Lambton. Basing himself in Arkona from 1861 to 1901, he conducted a branch in nearby Forest from 1882 until 1890. *AC*

The Old Van Tuyl & Fairbank Hardware Store, Northeast Corner of Petrolia Line & Station Street, Petrolia, circa 1930

Undoubtedly, the county's most famous nineteenth-century retailer was Van Tuyl and Fairbank. Established in 1865 by John Henry Fairbank and re-organized in 1873 with the naming of Benjamin Van Tuyl as a partner, the store did a brisk business in outfitting the area's oil industry with drilling tools, specialized light machinery, piping, well pumps, valves, casings, and a variety of more conventional hardware, including nails, screws, nuts, bolts, hinges, flanges, hooks, locks, and sheet metal. Of course, the firm also courted the lucrative farm and building supply trades. During the peak of Petrolia's oil boom in the late 1880s and early 1890s, the Van Tuyl and Fairbank business, as Lambton's premier merchandiser, was estimated to be worth approximately $200,000 (around at least the $3,000,000 mark in today's terms). However, local success was only partly responsible for the establishment's renown. Indeed, since Petrolia's foreign drillers carried the firm's products to oil fields throughout the world, Van Tuyl and Fairbank enjoyed worldwide sales recognition. *LCL*

OPERATING ROOM
HADDENS ART STUDIO
ALVINSTON ONT

Interior of George A. Hadden's Photo Studio, Alvinston, circa 1905

Although itinerant photographers may have made earlier local appearances, we can trace professional studio photography in Lambton back to 1852, the year that David B. Wawanosh, chief of the Sarnia Chippewas, opened a daguerreotype gallery in Port Sarnia. While Wawanosh stayed in business for only a few years, his establishment heralded the arrival of a trade that spread across the county over the next decade and a half.

Hailing from Detroit, George A. Hadden operated a photographic studio in Alvinston from 1899 until 1922 and maintained branch studios in Thamesville (1902 to 1903) and Brigden (1908 to 1919). Typical of the small-town photographers of his day, he derived most of his income from portraiture. Indeed, to ensure a steady stream of sitters before his camera, he routinely lowered his prices to such a degree that he lured customers from all over the Lambton-Kent-Elgin-Middlesex region. Enterprising by nature, he expanded into the picture-postcard line as soon as postal regulations were modified in 1903 to allow the mailing of postcards. In many respects, Hadden's photo-postcards are his greatest legacy. He produced hundreds of Lambton images, some of which appear in this book, including the scene above. *AC (George A. Hadden photo)*

Keating & Perry Newspaper Office, Oil Springs, circa 1865

As commercial enterprises, Lambton's newspapers have lived or died by the health of their advertising revenues and circulation levels. However, particularly during the nineteenth century, political opinion was the driving force behind the journalism business. Indeed, one of the county's earliest newspapers, *The Samiel*, published at Errol in the mid-1840s, hurled inky vitriol at Malcolm Cameron and his supporters in Port Sarnia for using their political connections to have their village, rather than Errol, selected as the terminus for the plank road from London. Moreover, in keeping with the spirit of the times, one could usually find a Liberal and a Conservative newspaper in the same urban centre. For instance, Petrolia had the *Topic* (Grit) and the *Advertiser* (Tory). Not surprisingly, these two journals agreed on very little, including the spelling of their town's name. The *Topic* wrote it as Petrolea, while the *Advertiser* put it as Petrolia. However, harmony did not always exist within each political camp. For instance, in the columns of his *Lambton Shield*, Alexander Mackenzie so harshly denounced fellow Liberal Malcolm Cameron that the latter sued the future prime minister for libel in the early 1850s. Cameron won the suit, and for financial reasons Mackenzie was forced to cease publication.

County newspapers were also political in that they promoted and defended the economic interests of their communities. Besides *The Samiel*, notable in this regard was Keating and Perry's *Oil Springs Chronicle*, a broadsheet which, for obvious reasons, gave due attention to local and international oil news. By the way, this boomtown paper of the 1860s was Lambton's first daily. *LCL*

Lambton Mutual Annual Report, 1895

Financial institutions played an important part in the county's nineteenth-century economic advancement. By loaning money, banks, trust companies, loan companies, building societies, and private lenders essentially channelled surplus capital (saved monies) to where it was needed for development. At the other end of this cycle, insurers secured invested capital against loss by fire, accident, or disaster. Mutual insurance companies – so called because their policyholders divided a portion or all of the annual profits amongst themselves – were significant providers of this service in rural Victorian Canada. Since these organizations kept local money in the community, their establishment was most likely rooted in the pragmatic financial conservatism that characterized the nation's agricultural areas.

In 1875, farmers from Bosanquet, Warwick, Brooke, and Euphemia formed a mutual insurance company. The next year, they merged with a similar group from the county's six other townships to create the Lambton Farmers' Mutual Fire Insurance Company. This enterprise limited its risks to rural schools, rural churches, and agricultural property, such as farmhouses, outbuildings, and livestock. Above all, however, the company expected its policyholders to follow a strict code of fire safety measures that called for, among other things, no smoking in barns, the vigilant operation of steam-powered thresher engines, and the proper maintenance of stoves and ovens. Interestingly, by exacting such restrictions, mutual insurance companies contributed to overall farm improvement. At any rate, as the figures quoted in this document attest, local farmers obviously did not find these policy conditions too onerous. Headquartered at 7873 Confederation Line in Watford and now known as the Lambton Mutual Insurance Company, the business still proudly serves county residents. *Lambton Mutual Insurance Company*

INDUSTRY

The Point Edward Fishery, from the Canadian Illustrated News for January 1, 1876

A striking feature of modern Lambton is the enormity of the enterprises in Canada's Chemical Valley. Not as immediately obvious are the colossal amounts of capital that built and keep these plants in operation. These prominent characteristics of the area's modern industrial landscape stand in sharp contrast to the relatively inauspicious beginnings of local industrial heritage. Indeed, since the capital required to develop large-scale secondary manufacturing far outstripped the economic capacity of nineteenth-century frontier societies, natural resource extraction and agricultural manufacturing formed the foundations of Lambton's early industrial sector.

Commercial fishing along the Lake Huron shoreline ranks among the county's first industrial activities. In the early 1830s, Henry Jones ran a modest herring operation near the site of present-day Point Edward. In 1838, John P. Slocum, an American from New York state, assumed control of this fishery. After Slocum's death in 1849, first his son and then the Hitchcock family carried on the business. The commercial fishery further north along the lake did not get its start until much later in the nineteenth century.

When the above illustration was first published, the Point Edward fishery had long been supplying local and eastern markets with thousands of barrels of fish per year. The season usually began in April after the months-long freeze-up on Lake Huron had ended. Hauled in by hand from the beach, seine lines of up to 2,500 yards (2,250 metres) yielded catches of herring, pickerel, and whitefish. After being opened and cleaned manually, the fish were packed into brine-filled barrels and then carted off to railway cars for shipment. Today, with much more sophisticated and mechanized techniques, Purdy Fisheries Limited, based just south of the Blue Water Bridges, works the Point Edward fishery. *JJTRC*

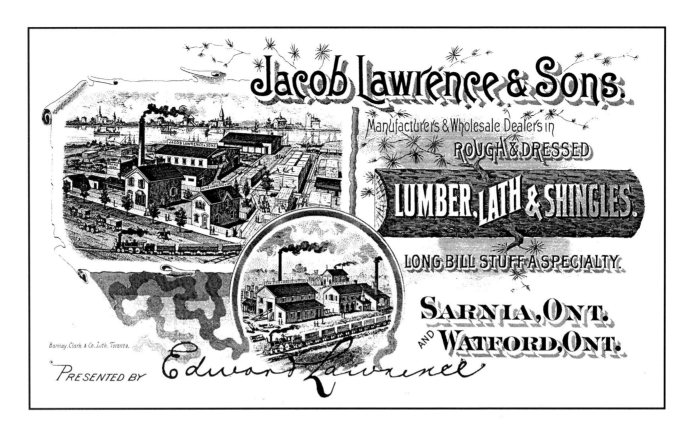

Coultis Saw Mill, Thedford (opposite top), circa 1900,
Hayne Milling Company, Brigden (opposite bottom), circa 1920
& Jacob Lawrence and Sons Calling Card, Sarnia & Watford (above), circa 1895

Given that forests once blanketed much of Lambton, it is not surprising that lumbering and saw milling loomed large in the local economy during the nineteenth and early twentieth centuries. In 1871, for instance, the wood processing industry employed nearly half the county's industrial workforce and accounted for just over one-quarter of the total value of Lambton's industrial output.

Manufacturers of squared timbers, deals, planks, boards, staves, barrel headings, lath, shingles, planed stock, and milled goods for local and exports markets, the Coultis, Hayne, and Lawrence operations were typical of the dozens and dozens of saw milling businesses that once covered the county. While the former two relied heavily upon Lambton's interior for their trees, the latter established a branch in Sarnia in order to process booms of logs floated down Lake Huron from Georgian Bay. Each established during the third quarter of the 1800s, all three concerns lasted well into the twentieth century. Indeed, the Coultis mill presently continues as one of Thedford's industrial mainstays. *LHM, AC, LHM*

Wellington roller mills.
Shetland near Bothwell Ont. av.

Wyoming Woolen Mills,
A. G. SYERS, PROP.,
MANUFACTURER OF
Tweeds, Full Cloths, Plain and Fancy Flannels,
Shirtings and Stocking Yarn.

Manufactures 10,000 Yards of Cloth annually. Custom Carding, Spinning,
Weaving Cloth Dressing, &c., executed with dispatch.
Wool bought or taken in Exchange at WYOMING MILLS—best in the
County of Lambton.

Wellington Roller Mills, Shetland, 1908
& Directory Advertisement for the Wyoming Woolen Mills, 1877

Until just after the Second World War, most manufacturing activity in the county was in some manner connected to agriculture. Notable in this regard are historic grist mills. Processing locally grown grain into flour and meal, they once lined Lambton's creeks, streams, and rivers, the currents of which were initially harnessed as sources of power. Aside from anchoring the industrial development of early urban settlements, these businesses served as vital economic links between the farming community and the export trade in milled grains. To this end, prior to the Great Depression of the 1930s, a great deal of flour and meal produced in the county found its way to eastern Canada, the United States, and Britain. The Wellington Roller Mills, operating on the banks of the Sydenham River during the late nineteenth and early twentieth centuries, gave farmers in the southeast corner of Lambton access to these distant markets.

As processors of sheep's wool into yarn and a variety of fabrics, woolen mills also contributed to the local agricultural economy; however, stiff competition from elsewhere and the county's relatively modest sheep herds curbed the proliferation and success of this industry in Lambton. Nevertheless, woolen mills in Watford, Thedford, Sarnia, Florence, Arkona, and Alvinston, along with A.J. Syers' Wyoming Woolen Mills managed to find sufficient market niches for survival during the last third of the nineteenth century. Still, the rise of absolutely monstrous mills in Toronto, Ontario's east, and Montreal ultimately spelled the doom of the industry in Lambton. By 1915, all but the Dickison establishment in Arkona had ceased production. The Sarnia Woollen Mills lived on in name only as a retailer of clothing and dry goods. *LCL, AC*

Forest Basket Company Truck, 1930

Not all agriculturally based manufacturers in the county were food processors. For instance, the Forest Basket Company Limited, established in 1913, produced a variety of baskets, crates, boxes, and hampers for the fruit, vegetable, and meat-packing industries in Lambton and across Southwestern Ontario. Employing a yearly staff of approximately 80 to 100 people, with an extra 50 or so hired for summertime peaks, the plant boasted a daily manufacturing capacity of 30,000 berry boxes, 10,000 eleven- or six-quart fruit baskets, or 7,200 bushel baskets. Naturally, with these production levels, the factory needed its own trucks for timely shipment. However, as a qualifying trailer on company letterhead noted during the 1930s: "All orders and agreements contingent upon strikes, fires, accidents and other delays unavoidable beyond our control." At any rate, the Forest Basket Company stayed in business until closing in the spring of 1968. Subsequently reopened, the factory shut down for good five and a half years later. *LHM*

Cheese Factory, Brooke-Warwick Township Line, Just South of Watford, circa 1895

The commercial cheesemaking business did not get its start in Ontario until 1864, when the province's first cheese factory opened near Norwich in Oxford County. This initial experiment proved a success and the industry quickly spread across Ontario's southern counties over the next decade. Around the turn of the nineteenth century, dairy farmers were supplying milk to nearly two dozen cheese factories in Lambton, including this one pictured above. While these enterprises sold some of their products locally, they mostly participated in Canada's booming export trade in cheddar. The principal market in this economy was Great Britain. However, Canadian cheesemakers met increasingly fierce challenges within the

Empire for British sales. As events turned out, Canada, and therefore Lambton, lost significant market share to, of all places, New Zealand. By 1915, stiff international competition, as well as brisk consolidation within the Canadian industry, had winnowed the number of cheese factories in the county down to the Brigden Cheese and Butter Company and H.W. Hamilton's plant in Thedford. L to R - unidentified, Dan Kelly, Fred King, unidentified, Harry Green (apprentice cheesemaker in doorway), unidentified, Ben Richardson, ? McKeune (factory manager), unidentified, Jim Henderson (standing on wagon behind boy), Alvin Maitland, unidentified, unidentified. *LHM*

Butter Wrapper,
Lambton Creamery, Petrolia, circa 1940

While international and domestic dynamics of trade thinned out the ranks in Lambton's cheesemaking industry, commercial milk processing began its ascendancy. Undoubtedly putting to rest the anxieties of local dairy farmers, this business trend sprang from a set of interrelated factors. Around the turn of the nineteenth century, the interplay between an increasing standard of living and widening knowledge about the dietary and health needs of both children and adults fostered rising demand, particularly in urban centres, for the efficient and sanitary delivery of milk. Each producing milk from their own cows and each directly hauling the same to customers, dairy farmers were simply not capable of individually responding to the task. Unwilling to ignore the possibilities of a changing world, they instead pooled their resources to form corporate dairies and creameries. (Technically speaking, a creamery was defined at the turn of the century as a factory where butter was manufactured. However, since many also dealt in fluid milk, creameries often operated as dairies in the conventional sense.)

Established in 1902, the Lambton Creamery Company was one of the county's first corporate dairies. It operated in a local industry that at various times included milk plants in Alvinston, Watford, Forest, Ravenswood, Oil Springs, Wyoming, Brigden, and Sarnia. Besides butter and bottled milk and cream, the Lambton Creamery sold eggs, cheese, ice cream, and, on a limited scale, garden produce. The company also rented cold storage space to the general public. In 1943, in what was likely a measure to strengthen itself against the threat posed by the aggressive giant of Ontario's dairy industry, Silverwood's of London, the Lambton Creamery expanded to Wallaceburg and changed its name to Lambton-Kent Creameries. The move initially gave the company some room to breathe. However, over time, Silverwood's proved to be too strong. Amid stiff competition, the Petrolia enterprise closed in the early 1960s. *LHM*

"Butter is a Natural Food"

REG. NO. 860
ONE LB. NET WEIGHT

Lambton Brand
Creamery Butter

CANADA FIRST GRADE

LAMBTON CREAMERY CO.
PETROLIA

Catalogue Cover, Watford Implement Works, circa 1880

A great deal of early heavy manufacturing in the county was also tied to agriculture. For example, makers of farm machinery had obvious links to the rural economy. Without question, Lambton's most renowned Victorian industrialist was the proprietor of the Watford Implement Works, Thomas Doherty. During his early working life as a farmer and blacksmith in Uttoxeter, he learned a pair of lessons that later served him well over the course of his business career. One, he grew to appreciate the needs and concerns of the farming community. Two, he came to understand the properties of iron and steel.

In 1876, Doherty established the Watford Agricultural Implement Works. To guide this business, he called upon his knowledge of farm life. Besides tinkering with improvements to everything from plows to reapers, he invented his own threshing machine. As was the promotional custom, Doherty routinely displayed his wares at a host of local, regional, and provincial fairs and exhibitions. Rapidly building up a remarkable record of prize winnings, he saw sales at his factory boom. However, a restless spirit marked the man, and he left Watford in 1882 to launch a stove foundry in Sarnia. Doherty put the management of his Watford plant in the capable hands of a recently acquired partner, David Thom.

Sarnia's Doherty Manufacturing Company enjoyed substantial success, as its stoves found customers across the breadth of Canada. Moreover, its president further demonstrated his inventive talents. In 1890, he patented a hot water boiler system, and at the turn of the century, he constructed two automobiles of his own design. The first one was powered by a coiled spring and the second by a gasoline engine. However, what truly distinguished Doherty was his development of an entirely new and efficient method of casting metal. Announcing his "Ferrous Steel" process in 1894, he commanded worldwide attention in metallurgical circles. A few years later, Doherty sold the rights to his invention for $650,000 (worth at least a dozen times that in today's terms). *LHM*

ENNISKILLEN
OIL REFINING COMP'Y,
OIL SPRINGS, C.W.

The Best Refined Oil always on Hand.   All Orders promptly attended to.

E. C. BRADLEY, Agent.

Directory Advertisement, Enniskillen Oil Refining Company, 1864 & James Miller Williams, circa 1875

Few counties in Canada have ever owed so much to a single individual than Lambton has to James Miller Williams. Taking his cue from the failed dreams of others who had attempted to exploit the oily gum beds in south-central Enniskillen Township, the carriage maker from Hamilton, Canada West dug into the beds to find their source. In 1858, he found the source alright, and his oil well, the first commercial one in North America, triggered a long and exciting chain of events that redirected the entire course of the county's history. Indeed, everything from the eventual rise of Petrolia to the establishment of Imperial Oil to the development of Chemical Valley, Canada's largest complex of petrochemical refineries, can be traced to Williams' modest quest.

Of course, in the more immediate scheme of things, his discovery touched off the oil boom which saw the birth of Oil Springs. Lured by the promise of fast and immense riches, fortune-seekers, such as E.C. Bradley, poured into the village. Indeed, at one time during the early 1860s, the municipality's population was claimed to be as high as 5,000 or 6,000 residents. Unfortunately, the local oil fields soon betrayed their fame. By the late 1860s, they had been largely tapped out, and the boom naturally turned to bust. However, many of those who abandoned Oil Springs, including the intrepid agent of the Enniskillen Oil Refining Company, merely relocated to another boomtown founded on the "greasy." Only several miles further north, that place was Petrolia. *AC, LCL*

John D. Noble's Oil Wells, Petrolia, from the Canadian Illustrated News *of February 11, 1871*

In contrast to Oil Springs, Petrolia enjoyed significantly larger oil reserves. This blessing afforded the oil industry in Petrolia a greater measure of stability and permitted the development of some immense operations. As the *Canadian Illustrated News* marvelled at the success of one local oil barron: "John D. Noble is one of the most enterprising oil producers in Canada, and has done very much towards lessening the cost of the production of crude oil by consolidating the machinery and appliances therefor under one building [pictured above] for the purposes of pumping several wells with the same amount of labour and fuel... Mr. Noble employs about thirty men a day at his works, has fifteen steam engines in operation, and about 20,000 feet of tubing or iron pipe for conveying the oil, and about 30,000 barrels of tankage capacity for holding the same... Mr. Noble estimates the total production of his wells to be about 700 barrels per week, which is about 1/10th of the total production of the oil wells of Canada." *JJTRC*

"Shooting" an Oil Well, Petrolia, circa 1905

Sinking or "shooting" a oil well in the Petrolia oilfields was essentially a three-step process. First, the oil workers, proudly billing themselves as Hard Oilers, manoeuvred a drilling rig over a predetermined spot and began to bore a hole into the ground. If the fissile shale that crowns most of Lambton's oil deposits refused to crack – and it was often that uncooperative – the drillers next resorted to using locally manufactured explosives to force open the stubborn rock. Packed into large metal tubes known as torpedoes (left), these charges were usually made of dynamite or some other nitroglycerine-based product. Upon the subterranean detonation of a torpedo or two, the shale yielded its treasure in a rumbling burst of excitement (right). Finally, the Hard Oilers triumphantly capped the gusher.
Archives of Ontario (John Boyd photos)

Imperial Oil Office, Petrolia, circa 1895 & Canadian Oil Refinery, Petrolia, circa 1905

In 1880, a group of leading Canadian oil producers, among them Petrolia's Jacob Englehart, incorporated the Imperial Oil Company Limited. Initially, Imperial maintained its headquarters and chief refinery in London, then one of the country's major oil refining centres. However, after a fire virtually destroyed the London works three years later, Imperial decided to transfer its head office and principal refinery to Petrolia. Aside from furthering the town's already sound economy, these moves confirmed Petrolia as king of Canada's oil industry. However, the high times would soon end.

In 1897, Standard Oil, the American colossus, swallowed up Imperial. After the takeover, Standard determined that Sarnia, with its waterfront advantages, would make a better home for its new acquisition. The next year, Imperial moved to the port town. Not only was the relocation a tough knock to Petrolia's prestige – after all, it had lost out to its chief municipal rival in Lambton – it was also a serious blow to the local economy, especially since, making matters even worse, the oilfields were then showing ominous signs of giving out. As census returns reveal, both circumstances were truly awful for

Petrolia. In 1891, for instance, the value of goods manufactured in the town (mostly oil products) was $1,983,100. Ten years later, the annual figure had plummetted to $261,493.

Many Hard Oilers left Petrolia for work in oilfields across the globe or went with Imperial to Sarnia. Some found jobs in other industries, and others retired altogether. But, unlike many other boomtowns, Petrolia refused to dwindle into oblivion. Rather, it built itself back up by diversifying its industrial economy. New enterprises, such as the Lambton Creamery, the Petrolia Wagon Works, the Petrolia Pork Packing Company (later a cannery), and the Petrolia Bridge Company, helped to fill the void left by Imperial's departure. By 1911, the value of Petrolia's industrial products had rocketed to $1,167,791, a near quintupling since the dismal return of 1901. However, the town did not entirely break with its past. Refining what local oil remained, as well as imported oil pumped in from Froomfield, the Canadian Oil Refining Company, incorporated in 1901, was another concern that powered Petrolia's recovery during the early twentieth century. *JJTRC, AC*

Polymer Refinery, Sarnia, circa 1960

Although the monstrous Imperial Oil works at Sarnia marked the municipality as Canada's new oil refining capital, it was not until the Second World War that what grew to become Chemical Valley truly got its start. By 1941, Japanese military conquests had largely cut off the Allies from the vast rubber tree plantations in the South Pacific. The Allies' only other natural rubber sources, particularly in South America, were simply incapable of satisfying the war effort's hurried demand for rubber products. The only alternative left was to develop a large-scale manufacturer of artificial rubber, a feat which had not yet been accomplished in the private sector.

C.D. Howe, Canada's Minister of Munitions Supply, selected Sarnia as the logical spot for the experimental plant. Time was of the essence, and the city, as home to Imperial Oil and Dominion

Salt, could readily supply the proposed plant with essential feedstocks and brine. In addition, Dow Chemical of Midland, Michigan was invited to build a local facility in order to supply the new refinery with styrene.

In June of 1942, construction began on the complex eventually known as Polymer Limited (later Polysar, then Nova, and now Bayer). A little more than a year later, in what was an amazing feat of engineering, the refinery opened. After the war, the plant continued to operate and, indeed, later expanded. Significantly, the cluster formed by Polymer, Dow, and Imperial Oil lured a host of other petrochemical giants to the area during the 1950s and 1960s, and thus Chemical Valley was born. *AC*

Dawn Station, Ontario Natural Gas Storage and Pipelines Limited, Bentpath Line at Cuthbert Road, West-Central Dawn Township, July 18, 1960

When oil drillers fanned out from Enniskillen in search of the "greasy" throughout Ontario, they located pockets of natural gas under Dawn, Euphemia, Moore, and Sarnia Townships, Oil Springs, the city of Sarnia, and, for that matter, Kent and Essex Counties. Discovered just prior to the First World War, Dawn's gas deposits turned out to be Lambton's most lucrative. Over the next few decades, the fuel from under the township was piped to customers across Southwestern Ontario. After the Second World War, when the reserves were showing signs of significant depletion, Ontario Natural Gas Storage and Pipelines converted the exhausted gas wells into a seasonal storage complex, into which natural gas from Alberta, Texas, and local wells was pumped during the summer for use during wintertime peaks. Today, Union Gas uses the Dawn facility as an integral part of its distribution network in Southern Ontario. *Archives of Ontario (Ministry of Trade and Tourism photo)*

Aerial View of the Elarton Salt Works, Warwick Township, circa 1960

Salt was another gift from the county's geologic past that Victorian Lambtonites discovered amidst their frenzied quest for oil. In 1870-71, brothers Charles and Arthur Kingstone established Lambton's first commercial salt block on the south side of today's Lambton Line between Kingscourt and Salt Roads in Warwick Township. Named the Elarton Salt Works, the enterprise used the brine method to mine the salt bed that was formed by the Devonian sea which covered what is now the Great Lakes basin 405 million years ago. Ingenious in its simplicity, the brine method called for the injection of water into the salt layer 1,400 feet (420 metres) below soil level. After the water had dissolved the mineral, the resulting solution was pumped up to the surface where it was put through an evaporation process. Once the water had been removed, crystalized salt was all that remained.

The Elarton Salt Works enjoyed a very successful beginning and even captured a silver medal at the Paris International Exhibition of 1878. However, competition from other salt plants, including those at Port Franks, Sarnia, Mooretown, Courtright, and outside the county, increasingly challenged the Warwick business. It closed for the first time around in 1900. Sporadically revived for brief periods during the 1920s, '40s, '50s, and '60s, the mine shut permanently in 1970. *LHM*

Sifto Salt Advertisement, 1915 & Mooretown Salt Block, circa 1905

Moore Township has been home to four salt businesses. Courtright had a salt block from the mid-1880s until 1928, and during the early 1900s, A.A. Bedard, proprietor of the Courtright Hotel, bottled the brackish, yet salubrious waters he had tapped beneath his inn. The Mooretown Salt Company, billing its salt as "Ontario's purest," operated from 1890 until amalgamating with the plant at Courtright in 1912. Meanwhile, another salt block stood just north of Mooretown around the turn of the nineteenth century.

Sarnia's Dominion Salt Company originally began as the Empire Salt Company in 1904. Six years later, the Cleveland-Sarnia Saw Mills sold its interest in Empire to the parties who formed Dominion Salt. Ranking as Lambton's largest salt works, Dominion enjoyed a profitable half century on Sarnia Bay until the deposits were practically exhausted in the mid-1960s. While mining ceased in 1964, the company left three enduring legacies. One, it sold its property to the City of Sarnia for use as a park, later named Centennial to commemorate Canada's one-hundredth birthday. Two, the vast caverns left by the brine operations have well-served Chemical Valley as underground storage facilities. And three, the Sarnia-based enterprise gave the country its most familiar brandname of table salt, Sifto, trademarked in 1914 by plant manager, Charles H. Rogers. *AC, LHM (Louis Pesha photo)*

Freight to the Upper Lakes.

THE *OLIVE BRANCH*, of Port Sarnia, will leave Kingston for Lake Erie, Rivers Detroit and St. Clair, and Lake Huron, about the 1st May, and will make regular trips throughout the season, as near monthly as possible. She is a safe, dry vessel, well appointed, and sails on "Teetotal Principles."

HOOKER, HENDERSON & Co..
Agents in Kingston.
MALCOLM CAMERON,
Agent at Port Sarnia.
Kingston, 19th April, 1842.

Advertisement for the Schooner Olive Branch, *from the Kingston Chronicle for May 14, 1842*

It should come as little surprise that inhabitants of a county blessed with a lengthy shoreline have long recognized the Great Lakes as a magnificent highway of commerce. Indeed, Lambton's marine advantages are what drew many leading settlers in the first place. For instance, the economic potential of the St. Clair River and its only natural harbour, the bay near its headwaters, strongly influenced one Malcolm Cameron of Lanark County to establish, promote, develop, and otherwise found a village on the river's edge. From this place,

named Port Sarnia in 1836, Cameron operated a fleet of schooners. Downbound, his sailing vessels, including the *Olive Branch*, carried Lambton's agricultural produce and manufactures to eastern markets. Upbound, Cameron's ships hauled imported and domestic goods from the east into the western frontier region. By the way, note that the *Olive Branch*, in keeping with its owner's commitment to the temperance movement, sailed on "Teetotal Principles." *UWO*

Port Franks Harbour, circa 1900 & Fuel Dock, Froomfield, circa 1965

In varying degrees of combination, stunted levels of early urbanization, limited access to capital, harbours naturally plugged with silt, and comparatively shallow shore waters prevented major ports from appearing on the county's Lake Huron coastline. Moreover, the draw of harbours blessed with official sponsorship and dynamic entrepreneurship, namely those at Goderich and Kincardine, kept Lambton's lakeshore relatively isolated from marine routes, and thereby further stifled lakeport establishment.

Port Franks, although now a busy recreational port, has a history strongly shaped by these factors. Initially, the Canada Company slated the place for harbour development. However, the company's designation of Goderich as the western seat of its settlement tract and primary port on Lake Huron and the ensuing influx of people and

capital into that town sharply downgraded plans for Port Franks. This, coupled with the fact that tons and tons of sediment were annually deposited at the mouth of the Ausable River – a circumstance that called for expensive dredging – sealed Port Franks' fate as a minor harbour.

Nevertheless, the St. Clair River provided Lambton with ample sites for port development. Indeed, even small places along the river seized opportunities in this regard. For instance, Froomfield has been home to a fuel dock since 1906. At first, this facility was employed to receive and pump oil from lake tankers to the Canadian Oil Company refinery in Petrolia. With the advent of diesel-powered ships during the 1950s and 1960s, the dock saw increasing use by Canadian Oil (later Shell) as a fuelling station. *LHM, AC*

P.W. Merritt & Son's Dock, Port Lambton, 1880

The dock of P.W. Merritt and Son was typical of the commercial wharves that jutted out into the St. Clair River during the nineteenth and early twentieth centuries. Steamboats, ferries, barges, rowboats, and even skiffs made regular calls at these docks to unload manufactured goods destined for direct delivery to riverside storekeepers or transshipment to landlocked merchants. Of course, consignments of agricultural produce and tree products were loaded aboard these craft. In particular, until the dominance of coal-fired ship boilers towards the end of the Victorian era, retailers along the St. Clair enjoyed a booming trade fuelling steam-powered vessels with cordwood harvested from the county's inland forests. Merchant docks, of course, also served the passenger trade. *AC*

Icelandic Immigrants at Point Edward, from the Canadian Illustrated News *for November 13, 1875*

As a logical staging point for marine access to the head of Lake Superior at either Thunder Bay or Duluth, Minnesota, Point Edward played a notable part in Western Canada's development. Destined for the Prairies, a tide of people and goods flowed through the port between 1872 and 1914. Upon arriving in Point Edward via the Grand Trunk Railway, they boarded the steamships of the North West Transportation Company and its corporate successor, the Northern Navigation Company, sailed to the Lakehead, and then travelled by rail into Western Canada. Even after Canadian Pacific inaugurated transcontinental service in the mid-1880s, the segmented western route through the Point remained busy. However, World War I abruptly ended the immigrant trade, although freighting continued. After the war, Point Edward's docks assumed prominence in the Great Lakes tourist trade.

Notable amongst the thousands who passed through the village on their way west were some of the first Mounties to be stationed on the Prairies. The Icelandic settlers pictured above were another fascinating group to stop in Point Edward. Bound for a new life on the shores of Lake Winnipeg, they established the town of Gimli, Manitoba shortly after this illustration was first published. *JJTRC*

 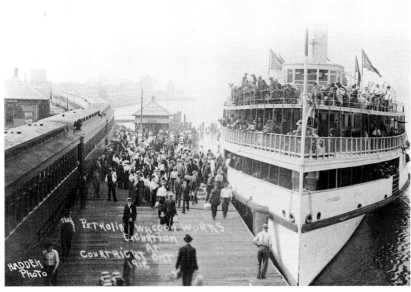

Sarnia Grain Elevator, circa 1960 & Michigan Central Railway Dock, Courtright, 1918

During the late nineteenth and early twentieth centuries, grain elevators stood along the banks of the St. Clair River at railway terminals in Courtright, Point Edward, and downtown Sarnia. However, while these three facilities were substantial in their own right and certainly enhanced local farmers' access to distant markets, the largest marine elevator to have ever existed in Lambton is the one that currently towers over Sarnia Bay. Built in 1927, the complex's original holding capacity was 1,000,000 bushels (as distinct from its annual processing capacity of several times more). Major expansions in 1928, 1941, 1952, and 1963 dramatically boosted its holding capacity to a colossal 6,000,000 bushels, making it one of the biggest elevators on the Great Lakes. Having long augmented the agricultural economy in Southwestern Ontario, the Sarnia elevator remains busy to this day. Pictured at the left, taking on a load of grain, is the *Alexander F. Holley*, one of the longest-serving "whaleback" or "cigar boats" on the Inland Seas.

From about 1880 until 1940, Lambton's ports also actively participated in the Great Lakes tourist economy. In particular, St. Clair River docks from Port Lambton to Point Edward were the points of departure for steamship and ferryboat cruises up and down the river, into Lakes Huron and St. Clair, and to holiday destinations, such as Tashmoo Park on Harsen's Island, Stag Island, Detroit, or cottage enclaves along the Lake Huron shoreline. Depicted in the postcard image to the right are Petrolia Wagon Works employees boarding the sidewheeler *City of Toledo* at Courtright for a summertime day-trip along the St. Clair. Undoubtedly, the river's cool waters were a strong drawing card for these merrymakers. Despite being immensely popular during the first third of the twentieth century, the Great Lakes excursion trade eventually lost out to the automobile. Quite simply, people grew to prefer the freedom of recreational choice offered by this landlocked mode of transportation. *AC, LHM (George A. Hadden photo)*

"Fitting Out" the Huronic, Sarnia, April 2, 1910 (opposite) & the Noronic, Point Edward (above), 1946

Aside from blessing their communities with transportation advantages, ports boosted local fortunes in other ways. For instance, the Northern Navigation Company injected untold amounts into the economies of Sarnia and Point Edward in order to keep its steamers, most notably the palatial *Huronic, Hamonic,* and *Noronic,* running during the first half of the 1900s. Maintenance and operating costs included repair bills from annual spring "fit outs," towage fees, and fuel charges. Moreover, shipping activities directly or indirectly gave employment to sailing crews, dockhands, teamsters, warehouse labourers, and hotel workers (tourist lodgings and meals). Of course, supplying ships chanelled business to local printers (promotional and shipboard literature and stationery), laundries, hardware merchants, food wholesalers, bakers, dairies, and even pop makers. Finally, as the scene above demonstrates, county ports also played important roles in the recreational economy of juvenile society. *City of Toronto Archives (John Boyd photo), AC*

Captain A.M. Wright of the Northern Navigation Company, circa 1925

Of the thousands of Lambton residents of both genders who have worked on the Great Lakes since the county's beginnings, none, perhaps, was as charming as Captain Alfred Montgomery Wright. Born in Collingwood in 1871, Wright began his sailing career as an eleven-year-old cabin boy. Quickly working his way up the ranks, he received his ship master's certification in June of 1894. For most of his career, he was associated with the Northern Navigation Company, under whose colours he captained the following steamships: *Brittanic* (1902), *Atlantic* (1903), *City of Midland* (1904), *Collingwood* (1905), *Majestic* (1906-08), *Saronic* (1909-13), *Huronic* (1914-18), *Noronic* (1919-22), and *Huronic* (1923-27). Seconded to Canada Steamship Lines, Northern Navigation's parent company, he captained the *Valcartier* for the 1928 and part of the '29 shipping seasons.

Wright's navigating talents were remarkable and earned him respect throughout the lakes. During the Great Storm of 1913, for instance, he skilfully piloted the *Saronic* to safe harbour. In order to be closer to Northern Navigation's base of sailing operations, the captain left Collingwood in favour of Sarnia in early 1914. Five years later, his employer, conferring its highest honour, made him commodore of the company fleet. Sadly, Captain Wright's engaging and infectious smile prematurely disappeared from the Great Lakes on August 8, 1929, when he died from a brief, but severe illness. Crew members, ship officers, fellow captains, company executives, former passengers, and all of Collingwood and Sarnia deeply mourned his untimely passing. *AC*

Charlie Cattanach (on dock with both hands in pockets), circa 1910

The son of a Great Lakes ship captain, Charlie Cattanach of Sombra began his sailing career sometime during his late teens around the turn of the nineteenth century. As was tradition, he started off as a deckhand, but, undoubtedly wishing to follow his father's path, he gradually climbed up the ranks. By the year of his thirtieth birthday, he had become the wheelsman on the 545-foot *Henry B. Smith*, then one of the largest bulk carriers on the Lakes.

At 5:00 p.m. on Sunday, November 9, 1913, the *Smith* steamed out of Marquette, Michigan downbound with a load of iron ore. Fate did not look kindly upon the freighter's 23 hands that evening,

as they had set out into the beginning of the worst storm to have ever hit the Great Lakes. Half an hour after leaving port, the *Smith* disappeared from view of the shore. The ship and her crew members were never seen again. Indeed, even to this day, nobody knows exactly what happened to the vessel – just that the unforgiving natural horror had plunged it into the depths of Lake Superior. News of Charlie Cattanach's tragic death devastated the village of Sombra. Tearful sympathies poured out to Charlie's grieving family and to the families of the other 250 sailors who had perished in the Great Storm of 1913. *Sombra Township Museum*

GETTING AROUND

*William Bullick Blacksmith Shop, Uttoxeter, circa 1900
& Horse Dentist Advertisement, from the* London Free Press *Christmas Issue for 1886*

After two feet and a sturdy pair of boots, the next most common means of travel in Lambton prior to the 1920s was conveyance by animal. And by far, the most popular four-footed mode of transport during this period was the horse, although donkeys, mules, oxen, cattle, and even dogs could be ridden or used to pull carriages, wagons, carts, sleds, and sleighs. Of course, just as the auto service industry is crucial in our present automobile age, the "horse maintenance" industry loomed large in the past. Scattered across the county, hundreds of skilled farriers and blacksmiths, such as William

Bullick, ensured that animals were properly shod. Although fewer in number than professional horseshoers, veterinarians also did their part to keep beasts of burden on the road. However, horse dentists like John Phelan were a fairly rare breed. Nevertheless, when one seriously thinks about it, these specialists performed a valuable function. After all, while a malfunctioning carburetor would prevent your car from digesting its fuel, would not a set of badly decayed teeth make it impossible, or at least very difficult, for a horse to digest its fuel? *LHM, UWO*

Plank Road Toll Gate, Sarnia Township, circa 1920

Land grant terms and statute labour laws required early Lambtonites to construct and repair roads. However, road-travel in the Victorian county could be uncomfortable in the least and mortally hazardous in the extreme as a result of harsh weather, poorly drained soils, occasional lapses in fulfilling road maintenance duties, and, when municipal taxes later paid for roads, widespread reluctance to hike the public rates. Nevertheless, our predecessors adopted a solution to such problems: the private road.

Lambton's most prominent private road, the Sarnia to Florence Plank Road, was incorporated in 1853. Although actually designed to benefit Port Sarnia's economic position, its incorporators promoted the scheme as the best means to improve communication diagonally across the county. However, the road never reached southeast Lambton. Instead, the Enniskillen oil boom convinced its shareholders to extend their venture only as far as Oil Springs. While not serving interests beyond the oil region, the thoroughfare gave central Lambton access to a harbour and, as intended, allowed Sarnia to exert even more influence over its hinterland.

Interestingly, Plank Road was the last toll road to operate in Ontario before the official opening in 1997 of the Express Toll Route (provincial highway 407) across Toronto. In 1926, after seventy years in private hands, Plank Road became public when it was absorbed into the province's highway system. Today, its first historic stretch is preserved as Ontario Street in Sarnia. *AC*

River Ferry at Becher, circa 1910 & the Daldean at Sombra, circa 1960

Lambton's rivers, streams, and creeks stood as formidable obstacles to land travel. For instance, the Sydenham River-Black Creek water system limited the early progress of road building. In short, constructing and maintaining bridges were relatively expensive undertakings at a time when low population levels prevented townships from raising sufficient tax revenues to pay for such amenities. Indeed, the best way to cross inland waterways that blocked access to urban centres was to avoid them altogether. This is why some of the last settled parts of the county were those areas effectively cordoned off by watercourses. This is not to say that our ancestors always conceded victory to the natural vagaries of geology. As their communities matured, they could afford the luxury of bridges. And where waterways proved too wide for conventional bridges, entrepreneurs established ferrying businesses.

Two types of ferries saw service in Lambton. Hand- or animal-powered craft were used in the county's interior, where moderate currents and narrow crossings rendered motorized power unnecessary. At the left is a typical example of this style of ferry. To traverse the Sydenham, its operator called upon his own muscle-power to pull the raft-like boat along a cable strung across the river. However, despite its simple efficiency, the Becher ferry was not renowned for comfort. As the sender of the postcard view wrote to the addressee: "Just a gentle reminder of wet feet." Meanwhile, the powerful flow and the tremendous breadth of the St. Clair River encouraged most ferry operators to rely on motorized craft that have ranged from small six-person motor-launches to much larger automobile ferries. The most famous of this last class of St. Clair ferry is the *Daldean*. Still going strong, it has carried millions of vehicles between Sombra and Marine City, Michigan since its launch in 1951. *LHM (Thomas L. Johnston photo), AC*

Grand Trunk Railway Yard, Point Edward, circa 1885

Victorians heralded the railway as their great conqueror of space and time. In contrast to other modes of transport, railways allowed them to travel over greater distances in less time and to do so in a more reliable fashion. Located on the western edge of Central Canada's population nexus and bordering the United States, Lambton was destined to enjoy rail connections. Indeed, as early as the 1830s, railway promoters in Toronto recognized the commercial advantages of laying track across the county in order to link their city with a rapidly growing American Midwest. However, it was not until the 1850s that rail lines finally reached into Lambton. In 1858, the first Great Western Railway train puffed into Sarnia from London. The next year, the Grand Trunk finished its Stratford-Point Edward route. In 1873, the Canada Southern belted mid-Lambton with its St. Thomas-Courtright branch. However, with the exception of their spur lines, these three railroads were east-west trunk lines. The county's only track with a north-south orientation was the Erie and Huron. Completed in the mid-1880s, it hugged the St. Clair River from Port Lambton to Sarnia. *AC*

Lowering the St. Clair Tunnel Shield into Place, Sarnia, mid-September 1889

The building of the St. Clair Tunnel between Sarnia and Port Huron, Michigan stands an absolutely marvelous feat of Victorian engineering. To overcome problems posed by oozing clay, soft gravel, and the occasional intrusion of water, project engineer Joseph Hobson chose the shield method to excavate the tunnel's route under the St. Clair River. Essentially acting like giant cookie-cutters, the two shields employed to dig the St. Clair Tunnel were each forced into the earth by twenty-four hydraulic rams. As the shields lurched forward, teams of labourers removed clay and gravel that collected within the giant metal cylinders. Aside from cutting into the soil, the shields prevented cave-ins at the digging points. Along the course of excavation, successive rings of cast-iron tunnel segments were bolted

into place. To minimize clay and water seepage, the emerging tunnel was pressurized at each end.

On August 30, 1890, after a year of digging, the shields met under the St. Clair. They were in perfect horizontal alignment and askew vertically by an inconsequential quarter inch. Rightly so, Hobson and his crew received worldwide recognition for their triumph over nature. The St. Clair Tunnel officially opened on September 19, 1891. At 6,025 feet, it was then the longest submarine tunnel anywhere on the globe. As an engineering wonder of its time, it gave lasting fame to Lambton County and, for that matter, to St. Clair County, Michigan. In the mid-1990s, a newly constructed tunnel supplanted the original one. *AC*

Railway Depots, circa 1910

Across the county, rail depots were central to urban and rural life. Through them flowed agricultural produce, manufactured goods, and the travelling public. In addition, since they handled the mails and usually doubled as telegraph offices, railway stations assumed prominence in the communications network of yesteryear. However, as county residents and businesses increasingly adopted automobiles and telephones, railways suffered from decreasing importance. Not surprisingly, this cycle of technological advancement sealed the fate of local depots. By the late 1980s, only Sarnia's railway station had escaped abandonment or falling into virtual disuse. Indeed, the old Great Western (absorbed by the Grand Trunk in 1882) and Erie and Huron routes are all that remain of Lambton's Victorian rail system. Clockwise from top left - the Michigan Central Railway (formerly the Canada Southern) depot at Oil City, the Grand Trunk Railway depot at Alvinston, and the Grand Trunk Railway depot at Petrolia (now the town's public library). *LHM (Louis Pesha photo), LHM, LCL*

The Hazards of Bicycling, Sarnia Township, circa 1905

The bicycle is an important, although generally overlooked Victorian contribution to modern transport. While first appearing in the late 1860s, it did not truly become a daily part of Canadian life until the 1880s and 1890s, when a mania for two-wheelers swept the entire Western World. Initially, riders had to contend with the hazards of the ordinary or "penny-farthing" bicycle. With huge front wheels and tiny rear ones, these contraptions were prone to throwing their masters for "headers" over the handlebars. However, in the early 1890s, the aptly named safety bicycle was developed. Having wheels of the same size and the diamond-shaped frame that remains popular to this day, the safety quickly replaced its more dangerous predecessor. By the mid-1890s, the Canada-wide bicycle boom was in full swing in Lambton. Thousands of county residents bought, traded for, manufactured, or even stole a "wheel" of their own. The craze continued into the twentieth century, when bicycles became so commonplace that comment about them faded into the background. Significantly, this form of transportation gave people a new-found freedom of travel. Of course, as amateur photographer John Boyd playfully reminds us, not everything about bicycle travel during his era was agreeable. By the way, just as this planet has more bicycles than automobiles, so does present-day Lambton County. Believe it or not! *Archives of Ontario (John Boyd photo)*

Maxwell Automobile, Watford, circa 1900 & White Rose Service Station, Reece's Corners, May 1, 1952

To date, no other form of transportation has had a greater influence upon modern society than has the automobile. Indeed, automobiles touch virtually every facet of our existence. If anything, we live in the automobile age – an age that began a century ago.

It may come as a surprise to some, but while the Fords, the Dodges, the Benzes, and other future international giants of the auto industry were starting or about to change world history, some Lambtonites were experimenting with automobile projects of their own. Around the turn of the nineteenth century, Sarnia industrialist Thomas Doherty invented two different cars (see page 80). And in 1900, after two years of tinkering, blacksmith and carriagemaker D.A. Maxwell appeared on Watford's streets with his automobile. Unlike Doherty's short-lived foray into auto manufacturing, Maxwell

kept his car operating well into the 1920s. In addition, for a few years beginning in 1912 and then again from 1920 until around 1930, Petrolia was home to a modest car factory.

While automaking did not take lasting root in Lambton, the auto service industry did. By the early 1920s, gas stations and garages were fairly common throughout the county. Naturally, as home to some of Canada's largest oil refineries, Lambton came to be associated with some of the country's most famous gasoline brandnames, including the White Rose line produced by Canadian Oil of Petrolia and later of Froomfield. Pictured to the right is the newly opened White Rose station in Reece's Corners. Still standing on the southeast corner of London Line and Oil Heritage Road, it is now a Petro-Canada franchise. *LCL, AC*

Sports & Recreation

Brigden Fair, circa 1930

The earliest fall fairs in Lambton were probably the ones held under the auspices of the St. Clair Agricultural Society during the 1840s. As the level of settlement in the county increased, rural exhibitions were organized on a township-by-township basis. The Moore Agricultural Society hosted its first fair in 1850. Like all rural fairs of the era, Moore's was chiefly a showing of livestock and produce. Of course, the fact that it centred around Philip Reilly's tavern on Lot 28, Concession 8 of the township suggests that sociability also figured prominently in the scheme of things. Indeed, it did, and the Moore fair grew in popularity and reputation. After alternating amongst the township's four villages, the fair finally settled upon Brigden as its home in 1889. In 1928, its directors decided to "open the prize list to the world." With this move, what had by then become widely known as the Brigden Fair confirmed its place as a major regional exhibition. A four-day fair since the mid-1980s, it still functions in much the same way fall fairs did a century and a half ago. Its considerable prize lists for agricultural and domestic accomplishments speak to its significant historical role in farming affairs. Meanwhile, its midway symbolizes the fair's notable heritage as an important social event. *LHM*

The Omar D. Conger *Dropping off "Merrymakers" at Stag Island, circa 1900*

During the last quarter of the nineteenth century, as the middle class found itself with increasing leisure time, an enduring vacation industry in Canada was established. In Lambton, a county blessed with a long freshwater shoreline, this new industry took firm root along the banks of the St. Clair River and the beaches of Lake Huron. In the 1890s, Nelson Mills, an expatriate Canadian living in Marysville, Michigan, founded a resort complex on Stag Island in the St. Clair. By the early 1900s, Stag Island tempted visitors with spacious cottages, a luxurious hotel, a large public dining hall, picnic grounds, a dancing pavilion, a baseball diamond, a half-mile bicycle track, nature trails, and some of the river's best fishing holes. However, life on the island was not entirely rustic – the vacation spot boasted its own steam waterworks, electric light plant, sewer system, and long distance telephone service to the outside world. These amenities combined to make Stag Island an extremely popular Great Lakes tourist destination during the Edwardian era. At the time the above photograph was taken, an adult could rent a cottage for $4.00 per week, seven nights' hotel board was $3.00 more, and a week's worth of meals cost $5.00. *Moore Museum*

Beach Scene, Grand Bend, circa 1935
& Ford Motor Company Picnic, Bright's Grove, circa 1930

Although many vacation camps and resorts were established along Lambton's Lake Huron shoreline at the turn of the nineteenth century, they did not truly blossom until after the end of the First World War. Initially, poor railway access hindered lakeside recreational development. However, with dramatic improvements to county roads and provincial highways during the 1920s and 1930s, the issue of accessibility faded away, and floods of tourists poured into Lambton's "west coast" each summer. Places, such as Grand Bend and Bright's Grove at each end of the county's lakefront, along with communities in between, including Errol, Blue Point, Hillsborough, Kettle Point, Ipperwash, and Port Franks, swelled with pleasure-seekers from all over the continent. Still powerful tourist draws, the county's Lake Huron communities have grown considerably over the past couple of decades with the arrival of year-round residents, many of whom had once made Lambton's lakeside their annual holiday destination. *LCL, LHM*

Boy Scout Troop, Brigden Train Depot, circa 1915

Organized recreational activities for youth in Lambton were not established in earnest until the very late nineteenth and early twentieth centuries. In essence, changing attitudes towards children brought about the recognition that youngsters also needed social channels through which they could express themselves while having fun. Of course, organized recreation for young people during this period was also designed to instil children with values. For instance, church and interfaith youth associations emphasized the duty of Christians to follow their faith. Sports clubs taught the worth of competition, fair play, and, quite naturally, physical exercise. Other youth organizations, such as the Boy Scouts and the Girl Guides, not only imparted life skills to their members, but also conveyed the importance of good citizenship and the value of self-reliance. *LHM*

Petrolia Citizens' Band, 1929

In an age before cassette decks, CD players, and the proliferation of radio, live musicians provided the public with most of its musical entertainment. These performers ranged in sophistication and taste from "one-man-bands" to string quartets to symphony orchestras. However, roughly between 1850 and 1950, brass bands reigned supreme. At the ready for parades, holidays, civic festivals, and private socials, these musical acts could be found in most Lambton communities during this period. One of the most talented brass bands to have ever played in the county was the Petrolia Citizens' Band. In 1927, '28, and again in '29, the Petrolians captured first prize for Class C1 at the Canadian National Exhibition's annual music competition. L to R - front: J.E. Campbell, J.L. Egan, Walter Thompson, Roy Anderson, William Taylor (bandmaster), Clayton Taylor, Charles Goldsmith, William J. Knight, William J. Thompson; middle: Joseph Gardiner, Jack Pepper, Frank Bolton, Thomas Truan, John Bell, Richard Sergeant, Robert Truan, H.L. Sanderson, H.G. McLean; back: W.B. Wilson, W. Cooper, N. Lindsay, J.S. Carroll, J.C. Thornton, J. Tillett, Elmer Kerr, Garnet Kerby, ? Molyneaux, A.C.H. Rippin (drum major), Wesley R. Thompson. *LCL*

The Alvinston Lawn Bowling Team, 1911

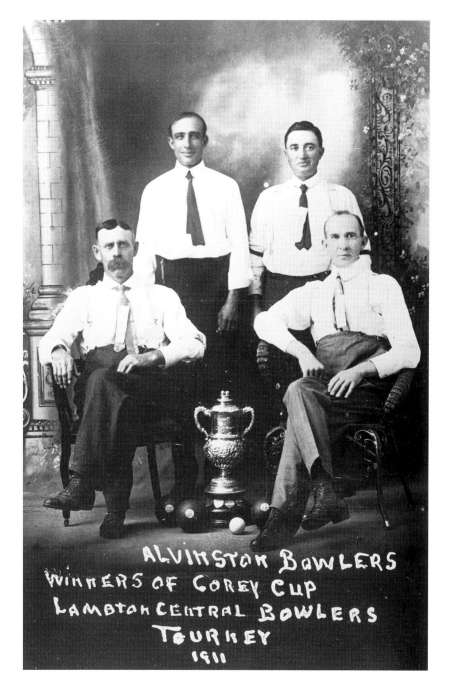

ALVINSTON BOWLERS
WINNERS OF COREY CUP
LAMBTON CENTRAL BOWLERS
TOURNEY
1911

During the early 1900s, the lawn bowling craze that swept through the Dominion found fertile ground in Lambton. By 1910, virtually every place of consequence in the county had at least one club. Unlike the three other major sports of the time — lacrosse, football, and ice hockey – lawn bowling was not physically punishing (although it could be mentally taxing at times). This decidedly genteel quality enhanced its appeal to those who were unable or unwilling to risk life and limb by playing Canada's more brutal games. However, what truly distinguished lawn bowling from other sports of the era was that many lawn bowling clubs had memberships open to persons of both genders. Still, the times being what they were, official lawn bowling tournaments were generally restricted to male participants. In the late summer of 1911, this quartet from Alvinston captured the Corey Cup as the victors in Lambton's premier lawn bowling competition. Unfortunately, gaps in our documentary heritage prevent us from discovering exactly who the Alvinstonians defeated to claim their trophy. *LHM (George A. Hadden photo)*

Petrolia's Ruby Football Team, Junior Champions of Canada for 1911

Despite Sarnia's football glory days of the 1920s and 1930s, Petrolia was Lambton's first powerhouse of gridiron talent. In the early 1900s, local teams in the Junior Division of the Ontario Rugby Football Union (ORFU) and from Petrolia High School dominated the game in Southwestern Ontario. Indeed, challengers from Sarnia were consistent fodder for the Hard Oilers during this era. Petrolia's pre-World War I zenith in football fortunes came in 1911. That year, after finishing the regular season with a perfect 4 and 0 record, the Hard Oil squad defeated the Hamilton Alerts 12 to 10 to take the Junior ORFU title. However, the team had to win two separate national championship games to claim Dominion honours. The first of these games was played on December 2 against the Hamilton Wanderers. The Petrolians bested their opponents from the Steel Town 15 to 8. But, since it was the great age of the "challenge game," the Hard Oilers had to answer the request sent by the team from Kingston's Royal Military College. Nevertheless, Petrolia, playing on home turf the next week, handily defeated the cadets 27 to 12. L to R - front: Frank Smith, Eddie Billings, George Deacon, Bloss Pollard, John Webb, Ted McGowan, Harry Crapper, Murray McQuien, Bob Webb; back: Jack Hartigan, Hugh Simpson, Jack Fisher, Ken Kerr, Con Peat, Sam Stokes, Charlie Bowen, George McPhedran, Ben Thomas, Alex McQuien, Jack Rainsberry, George Rose, Dave McMullen, Bruce Lackie, Harry Smith, Charles Fleming, Frank Perkins, Dr. C.O. Fairbank. *LHM*

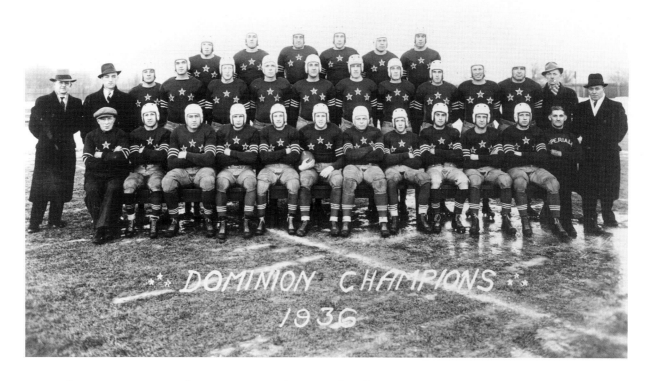

The Sarnia Imperials, Grey Cup Champions of Canada for 1936

Sarnians have never liked losing at sports, and they have especially hated to lose to any team from Petrolia. Not surprisingly, while Hard Oilers were capturing football honours during the early 1900s, a bitter seed was planted in Sarnia. That seed finally flowered in the 1920s, when a legion of great squads from Sarnia Collegiate Institute and Technical School (SCITS), fuelled by their impassioned rivalry with Petrolia, dominated football affairs not only in Lambton, but throughout Southwestern Ontario. As the '20s melted into the '30s, the cream of these SCITS players went on to form the core of the Sarnia Imperials, the local entry in the Ontario Rugby Football Union's Senior Division. As members of the "Imps," they contested for the 1933 Grey Cup, but lost in a 4 to 3 squeaker to the Toronto Argonauts. The next year, they captured the coveted trophy as Dominion champions by defeating the Regina Roughriders 20 to 12. The Imperials again brought home the Grey Cup in 1936 with a 26 to 20 triumph over the Ottawa Rough Riders. L to R - front: Walter Buxton, Rocky Parsaca, Orm Beach, Neil VanHorne, Mike Hedgewick, Gord Paterson, Cliff Parsons, Arnie McWatters, Keith Burden, Alex Hayes, Jim Geary, Bob Thorpe; middle: Bob Wyseman, Art Massucci (coach), Cal Moore, Jack Wickware, Ike Norris, Ralph Burr, Jack McLean, Bill Hall, Reg Ewener, Joe Woodcock, Len Rutter, Mike Clawson, Roy Brown, Roy Brush; back: Willie Kerr, Ken Stevenson, Claude Harris, Bummer Stirling, Red France, Pat Butler. *AC*

After the Tornado, Charles Mackenzie & Co., 144-46 North Front Street, Sarnia, July 13, 1879

Around 10:00 on the morning of Friday, July 11, 1879, the distant skies to the southwest of Sarnia filled with ominous purple-black clouds. The only relief to the approaching darkness was a massive lightning shower. By 11:00 a.m. it was apparent to Sarnians that a tornado was about to hit their town. Understandably, they scurried to find shelter. Fifteen long minutes later, the natural furry had passed, leaving in its trail a scene of utter chaos. Countless window panes were smashed. Roofs and chimneys had been ripped from their buildings, and lumber and "debris of every kind" had been strewn about. The most spectacular damage occurred along Front Street a few doors north of Cromwell. The entire roof of Robert and James Mackenzie's furniture warehouse on the westside of the street had been sucked up by the fierce winds and slammed against Charles Mackenzie's hardware store on the eastside. If any irony could be found in the storm's destruction, it was that the Mackenzies were all brothers. The twister also wrecked havoc in Point Edward and Port Huron, Michigan. In addition, its associated winds flattened two-thirds of the oil derricks in Petrolia and caused minor damage in Wyoming. Miraculously, the tornado claimed no human lives, although it seriously injured a few individuals. *AC (John Barron photo)*

THIS FACTORY IS 900 FT FROM MAGAZINE

EXPLOSION OF NITRO GLYCERINE PLANT OF "PETROLIA TORPEDO LTD" OCT 17 07

Nitroglycerine Factory Explosion, Petrolia, October 17, 1907

As home to several nitroglycerine plants (see page 83), Petrolia occasionally found itself in the newspaper headlines for what happened when nitro mixers made the rare mistake or two. Indeed, every one of Petrolia's nitroglycerine shops met the same, inevitable fate. Thankfully, technicians at these factories generally knew when they had erred, and thus they had a chance at self-preservation. Sadly, however, a few nitro workers were not so lucky in this regard.

At any rate, human nature being what it was (and still is), people were drawn to factory levellings in order to satisfy their pangs of morbid curiosity. As this widely circulated postcard view clearly indicates, the aftermath of the explosion at Petrolia Torpedo Limited was just such an event and even warranted posing in stylish dress before the photographer's camera. *LHM*

THE AUTOMOBILE ACCIDENT AT PETROLIA APRIL 8, 1915.

The Result of a Most Peculiar Automobile Accident, Petrolia, April 8, 1915

As a group of employees at the Canadian Oil Company readily discovered on Thursday, April 8, 1915, mechanical failure could be the cause of fairly bizarre automobile accidents. On that day, office staff members Lillas Riddell, Bessie Scott, Jim Clark, and Mr. C. Hales joined plant manager H.G. Tavener in the latter's Studebaker for a lunch trip into town. Once his passengers took their seats, Tavener began to turn his vehicle around. Unfortunately, the steering gear jammed just at the wrong moment, and instead of following the desired course, the car swung towards and then immediately plunged into an underground tank filled with eighteen feet of water and covered with a thick layer of crude oil. Not having time to escape, the Studebaker's occupants also went into the tank. Thankfully, some quick-minded onlookers rescued the unwitting swimmers by pulling them to safety as they bobbed through the oily scum. After numerous baths with generous treatments of "gasoline, coal-oil, hot suds, Old Dutch Cleanser, and every other modern dirt-chaser available," the adventurers returned to work a little worse for the wear, but much wiser for the experience. Undoubtedly, they settled upon a different lunch route and, perhaps, a different driver as well! *LHM*

The Sunken City of Genoa, Off the Foot of Davis Street, Sarnia, August 26, 1911

Navigation along the St. Clair River has always come with its perils. Early on the morning of Saturday, August 26, 1911, the steamer *City of Genoa* sailed into the St. Clair from Lake Huron. While this may seem routine, it should be noted that Captain McCulloch of the *Genoa* had ably piloted his craft through a dense fog into Sarnia Bay. Owing to the weather, he thought it best to anchor his ship until the fog had lifted. It was a sound judgement, but, as events turned out, McCulloch's problems were just about to begin. At 5:45 a.m., the steamer *W.H. Gilbert* rammed into the sedentary *Genoa*. With a giant hole stove in her side, the latter vessel sank like a rock in thirty feet of water. The *Gilbert* suffered only minor damage. Four weeks later, the *Genoa* was re-floated, but refused to let Sarnians forget her unhappy experience. Immediately rotting, the ship's waterlogged cargo of corn and grain filled the local atmosphere with an unbelievably awful stench. Given the right winds, the odour could be detected as far away as Point Edward and Port Huron, Michigan. *National Archives of Canada (John Boyd photo)*

The Burning Hamonic, Point Edward, July 17, 1945

Several spectacular ship fires have occurred along the St. Clair River, but none was as awesome as the burning of the Northern Navigation steamer *Hamonic*. Tuesday, July 17, 1945 began as a routine day for the ship's crew. However, a fire that engulfed the freight sheds next to the *Hamonic's* berth in Point Edward quickly leapt to the passenger liner. Despite imminent danger, Captain Horace Beaton managed to back his craft away from the burning dock and plow it into a spot of land just north of Purdy Fisheries and just south of the Century Coal Company's wharf. This bold move served two primary purposes. One, it removed the ship from the blazing shed and its blinding cloud of black smoke. Two, it kept the ship stationary so that rescue and firefighting efforts could be more effective. Elmer Kleinsmith, an employee of Century Coal, used the clamshell of his crane to hoist people off the *Hamonic's* top decks and lower them to the safety of dry land. Meanwhile, workers at Purdy's used fishing scows to ferry anxious passengers from the freight deck to shore. Also lending a hand, other boaters plucked from the water those who had jumped into the river. The fact that all 247 passengers and every crew member survived the fire illustrates that disasters can bring out the best in people. Reduced to nothing but a scorched shell, the once palatial *Hamonic* was later towed to Windsor and scrapped. *AC*

FAWCETT'S BANK,

WATFORD,

(ESTABLISHED IN 1871.)

Does a general banking business.   Issues drafts payable at par on the

BANK OF MONTREAL

And all its agencies.   Also gold and currency drafts on Smithers & Watson, agents of the Bank of Montreal, New York, payable at par in all the cities of the United States.

———

BRANCH OFFICES :

ARKONA—W. J. Ward, Clerk ; DRESDEN—Fawcett & Livingston ; WYOMING—T. Fuller, Clerk; and at Alvinston.

Thomas Fawcett, Banker, &c.

Directory Advertisement for Fawcett's Bank, 1877

In 1871, Thomas Fawcett established a private bank in Watford. Despite the vagaries of a severe economic recession, the banker was able to open branches in Alvinston, Arkona, Dresden, and Wyoming during the mid-1870s. In early 1883, the financial reporting house of Dun, Wiman and Company gave Fawcett its highest credit rating and estimated the pecuniary strength of his business enterprise to be somewhere between $75,000 and $125,000 (in an age when the average working man earned around $200 per year). However, appearances were quite deceiving, and in the very late summer of 1884, the bank failed. Hundreds of depositors in Lambton, Kent, and Middlesex Counties lost tens of thousands of dollars. Indeed, scarcely a neighbourhood in the eastern half of Lambton remained untouched by what was soon recognized as a financial scandal. At first the bank merely suspended payment, but then it closed entirely. To make matters worse for Fawcett's creditors, the bank's books disappeared and were later thought to have been burned. Without the ledgers, those who had lost their savings had slim legal means to recover their money. Instead, they settled for 4 3/4 cents on the dollar nearly three years after the bank shut its doors. Strangely, the books resurfaced about a year after the Fawcett estate had been wound up. As for Fawcett himself, he turned up several years later as the president of a bank in North Carolina. *LCL*

Images in Connection with the Finlay Murder, Sombra Township *(opposite)*
& Trial, Sarnia *(above), from the* Canadian Illustrated News *for November 27, 1875*

On Saturday, May 22, 1875, Sombra Township residents were shocked to hear that their neighbour, Ralph S. Finlay, had been found that day lying dead in his barn with an ugly gunshot wound to his head. At first it was speculated that Finlay had committed suicide. However, local gossip soon turned to suspicion that the "improper intimacy" between Finlay's wife, Ann, and his hired man, William Smith, had something to do with the death. When Mrs. Finlay and Smith failed to attend Finlay's funeral, mere hunches quickly hardened into confirmed beliefs. During the coroner's inquest held a few days later, Ann Finlay finally confessed that Smith had pulled the trigger and that she had known about it.

At Smith's trial, concluded in Sarnia on November 1, 1875, testimony indicated that at about 1:00 a.m on May 22, Smith intentionally annoyed a horse in order to draw his employer out to the barn. When Finlay stepped into the barn, Smith fired the gun. Found guilty, the murderer was sentenced to hang; however, his sentence was later commuted to life imprisonment. The next year, Ann Finlay also went to prison. Released owing to ill health, she died in Chicago sometime in July of 1879. Looking back on the sensational case in 1900, the *Sarnia Observer* reported that Smith had become "a raving maniac" at the Kingston Penitentiary "and now believes himself to be the Prince of Wales." *JJTRC*

MR. JUDGE MOSS.

MR. McMAHON, Q.C.

DAVID GLASS ESQ. COUNSEL FOR THE PRIS.

J.C. McARTHUR

FINLAY'S HOUSE &c SCENE OF THE MURDER OF MR. JOHN FINLAY, SOMBRA.

THE MURDERER SMITH.

MRS. FINLAY.

Summer Kitchen

Bed Room | Parlour | PANTRY

Bed Room | Bed Room

PLAN OF HOUSE

HOUSE TO STABLE

FOOT-PATH FROM

SOUTH & EAST VIEW OF STABLE, PIG-PEN & SHED

FRONT ELEVATION OF FINLAY'S HOUSE

BLACK HORSE | STALL

STALL

GREY HORSE STALL

BENCH

BLACK HORSE STALL

STALL

CHINKS

PLAN OF STABLE SHOWING POSITION OF BODY &c

NORTH END OF STABLE, SHOWING WINDOW BY WHICH THE MURDERER ENTERED.

Dusting for Fingerprints Immediately after the Oil Springs Bank Robbery, April 13, 1954

Surprisingly few bank hold-ups have occurred in Lambton over the last century and a half. However, one of the more notable ones took place at the Oil Springs branch of the Bank of Toronto during the afternoon of Tuesday, April 13, 1954. On that day, two robbers, each armed with a revolver, made off with $1,900 from the bank. Although an alert employee managed to set off an alarm bell, the pair, driving in a stolen car, managed to evade a police dragnet. Still, within twelve hours of the robbery, a remarkably quick and efficient investigation conducted by the Ontario Provincial Police resulted in the arrest of two men from the northern fringe of Kent County. Picked out of a police line-up by the bank's staff, the suspects then confessed to the crime. Subsequently tried and convicted, each of the accomplices was jailed for a term of two years less a day. *LCL*

PATRONS

The author and publisher would like to acknowledge the following for their interest in heritage matters and for their support of this publication:

Aberarder Central School
Donna E. Anderson
Peter Arthurs
Township of Brooke
Sylvia Bunker
Jean Fisher Cameron
George & Janice Cann
M.L. Clancy
Constance H. Clark
Cope Construction Company
Lawrence Crich
Bud & Marjorie Cundick
Patricia Davidson
Amy I. Dawson
Bonnie Donahue
Douglas Edgar
Marian Elliott
Bernice Fisher
Cheryl Fraser
Glenn Garrison
Laverne Goodhill
John L. Gordon
Gail Gravelle
Cheri Helps
Jean Heron
Doug Higgins
Leah E. Hill
Clarence Hodgson

Barb Huff
Bruce & Annabelle Jameson
Carolyn Jamieson
Kimcor Farms Ltd.
Ken Kingdon
Dorothea Knights
Rudy Krall
Lambton Branch O.G.S.
County of Lambton
Lambton County Historical Society
Lambton Mutual Insurance Company
Lambton Sesquicentennial Committee
Ellen M. MacKinnon
Jim Maitland
Christine Maniuk-Piggott
Russell Marsh
Mr. & Mrs. Blake E. Maxfield
Gene McCaffrey
Patricia M. McLean
Brian & Lynn McManaman
John McNeill
MIG Engineering Ltd.
David Mills
Maxine Miner
William P. Moran
Joan Nicholson
Bertha-Rose & Marshall Park
Don & Inez Pecena

Perch Lane Farms
Charles S. Phelps
Township of Plympton
Wanda Pratt
Janet Ramsay
Anne Randall
Darrell Randell
Gord & Jean Richardson
Marian & David L. Robinson
Carlyle Searson & Searson's Saw Mill
Noella Sharpe
Chris & Karen Slack
David W. Smith
Township of Sombra
Marilyn J. Steadman
R. Dean & Jean M. Stewardson
Jack C. Todesco
Bill & Patricia Truesdale
Union Gas Ltd. - Dawn Operations
Emile Varsava
Vision Nursing/Rest Home
Eric Walden
Allen R. Wells
Ray Whitnall
Dorothy Wight
Donald L. Williams
Leslea Williams
Mrs. Florence Wright

INDEX

accidents, 115-117
Ackland, Richard D., 40
Adams, William Dennis, 40
Adamson, Elizabeth, 65
Adamson, Lucy, 65
advertising, 68
agricultural progress, 58,63-64,72
agricultural statistics, 18,20,22,25,59,60
agriculture, 18,20,22,24-25,28,30,34,58-64,69,72,76-
    80,91,93,106
Alberta, 86
alcohol, 51
Alexander House, 52
Allen, John, 40
Alvinston, 16,35,51,70,76,79,103,111,119
American Revolution, 9
Americans, 12,39
Anderson, Archibald, 40
Anderson, Roy, 110
animals, 61,98,100
Annet, Velma, 47
architecture, 45,64
Arkona, 17,34,68,76,119
artificial rubber, 85
Atlantic (ship), 96
Auld, W., 64
Ausable River, 33,90
automobiles, 80,93,100,103,105,116,122
Aux Croches (village), 33

Bailey, James, 40
Bank of Toronto, 122
banks, 72,119,122
Baptists, 53
barn raising, 63
baseball, 107
baskets, 77
Bastard Township, 53
Bayer, 85
Beach, Orm, 113
beaches, 17,108
beasts of burden, 61,98,100
Beaton, Captain Horace, 118
Beattie, James, 40
Beatty, Mrs. W., 47
Becher, 100
Bedard, A.A., 88
Bell, John, 110
Bengough, J.W., 54
bicycle track, 107
bicycles, 104
Billings, Eddie, 112

Bird, John Jr., 40
Black Creek, 100
Black Creek Settlement, 30
blacksmiths, 80,98
Blue Point, 108
Blue Water Bridges, 73
Bobier, Arthur, 40
Bolton, Frank, 110
border patrol, 57
Bosanquet, Charles, 17
Bosanquet (Town of), 17
Bosanquet Township, 14,17,32-33,36,72
Boswell, Nathaniel, 28
Bowen, Charles, 112
bowling, 111
Boy Scouts, 109
Boyd, John, 104
Boylan, John R., 40
Bradley, E.C., 81
Bradley, William, 40
brass bands, 110
Brewer, J., 67
breweries, 51,57
Brewster (village), 33
Brewster, Benjamin, 33
Brewster's Mills, 33
Brichan, David, 40
Brigden, 28,70,74-75,78-79,106,109
Brigden, William Wharton, 28
Brigden Cheese and Butter Company, 78
Brigden Fair, 106
Bright's Grove, 108
brine method, 87
Britain/British, 8-9,11-13,15,21-22,25,39,48,61,76,78
Brittanic (ship), 96
Britton, Uriah, 40
Brock, Thomas, 30
Brooke, Lord, 16
Brooke Central School, 38
Brooke School Section #10, 38
Brooke Township, 14,16,19,28,34,38,72,78
Brotherhood of Locomotive Engineers, 46
Brown, Henry, 40
Brown, Robert, 40
Brown, Roy, 40
Brown, Thomas, 40
Brown, Wesley, 56
Bruce County, 16
Brush, Roy, 113
building trade, 69
Bullick, William, 98
Burden, Keith, 113

Burr, Ralph, 113
Burr, William, 40
business, 65-80,119
Butler, Pat, 113
butter, 78-79
Buxton, Walter, 113
by-laws, 36

Cairns, Helen, 47
Cameron, Malcolm, 14,20,26,54,71,89
Camlachie, 22
Campbell, J.E., 110
Campbell, M.S., 54
Canada Company, 17,33,90
Canada Southern Railway, 27-28,35,101,103
Canada Steamship Line, 96
Canada Temperance Act, 42,54-56
Canadian National Exhibition, 110
Canadian Oil Refining Co., 84,90,105,116
Canadian Order of Chosen Friends, 46
Canadian Pacific Railway, 92
Carr, James, 40
Carr, Mrs. J., 47
Carr, Mrs. S., 47
Carrol, Peter, 22,25
Carroll, J.S., 110
Cattanach, Charlie, 97
cattle, 61
Centennial Park, 88
Century Coal Company, 118
Chatham, 43
cheese, 78
cheesemaking, 78-79
Chemical Valley, 21,73,81,85,88
Chicago, 120
children, 109
Chippewas, 9-10,12,21,70
Chislett, John, 40
church groups, 46,109
City of Genoa (ship), 117
City of Midland (ship), 96
City of Toledo (ship), 93
Clark, Jim, 116
Clawson, Mike, 113
Clearwater (Town of), 23
Cleveland-Sarnia Saw Mills, 88
clubs, 46
coffins, 49
Colborne, Sir John, 19,21-23
Colborne, Lady, 22
Cole, Mrs. H., 47
Collingwood, 96

Collingwood (ship), 96
Collins, Charles, 50
Collins, Clare, 56
Colonial Office, 12
commerce, 26,65-72,119
Conservative Party, 41
constables, 40
Cook, Sidney F., 40
Cooper, W., 110
Corey Cup, 111
Cornell, John H., 40
coroner's inquest, 120
Corunna, 10,29,66
cottages, 93,107
Coulter, John, 40
courthouses, 39
Courtright, 27,61,87-88,93,101
Courtright, Milton, 27-28
Courtright Hotel, 88
Coutlis Saw Mill, 74,75
Craig, Helen, 47
Craig, Mrs. J., 47
Crapper, Harry, 112
creameries, 79
crime, 39-40,54,119-122
Crockard, Mrs. J., 47
Cronkhite, David, 40
crops, 60,62,76
Cullen, Peter, 40
custodians, 38
customs, 43

dairy produce, 78-79
dairying, 61,78-79
Daldean (ferry), 100
Dallas, John, 40
Dawn Township, 14,18,20,22,45,62,86
Dawn-Euphemia Township, 18,20
Dawson, Richard, 40
Deacon, George, 112
death, 49
Delmage, Arthur, 40
Demsey, ?, 38
Demsey, Edith, 38
Dennis, William Sr., 40
deportment, 44
Detroit, 43,70,93
Devonian sea, 87
Devonshire, 22
Diamond Jubilee, 48
Dickison family, 76
dining facilities, 107

disasters, 97,114-115,118
distilleries, 51,57
District of Hesse, 14
District of Moore, 14
divorce, 45
docks, 90-92,118
Dodds, Mrs. (Rev.), 47
Doherty, Thomas, 80,105
Doherty Manufacturing Company, 80
Dollier (explorer), 8
domesticity, 45
Dominion Alliance for the Total Suppression of the
  Liquor Traffic, 54
Dominion Day, 48
Dominion Salt Company, 85,88
Donald, Thomas, 40
Dover Township, 23
Dow Chemical, 85
drainage, 18,20,37
Dresden, 119
drinking, 51-57
Drope, A., 56
druggists, 65,68
du Luth (explorer), 8
Duke of Kent (Edward), 27
Duluth, Minnesota, 92
Dun, Wiman and Company, 119
Duncan, Mrs. B., 47
Durance, 31
Durand, George, 26
Durham, Lord, 15,29
dynamite, 54,83

Eastern Ontario, 76
Eastman, Joel, 40
Eastman, Nordale, 40
education, 38
Edward (Duke of Kent), 27
Egan, J.L., 110
Egremont, Lord, 25
Egremont Road, 10,22,25
Elarton Salt Works, 87
electricity, 107
Elgin County, 70
Elliotts, 64
Ellis, William, 40
Ellison, Richard, 40
Empire Salt Company, 88
engineering, 102
England/English, 11-12,15,22,39
Englehart, Jacob, 84
Enniskillen, Earl of, 19
Enniskillen Oil Refining Company, 81
Enniskillen Township, 14,19,30,41,81,86,99
Erie and Huron Railway, 29,101,103
Errol, 10,43,71,108
Essex County, 14,86
etiquette, 44

Euphemia Township, 14,18,20,22,64,86
Evans, Richard, 40
Eveland, Daniel, 40
Everest, George M., 68
Ewener, Reg, 113
excursion trade, 93
exploration (early), 8
explosions, 54,83,115
Express Toll Route, 99

fabrics, 76
Fairbank, Dr. C.O., 112
Fairbank, John Henry, 69
fairs, 28,80,87,106
Falone, Maurice, 40
farm improvement, 58,63,64,72
farm machinery, 62,80
farming (see agriculture)
farriers, 98
fashion, 44,45
Fawcett, Thomas, 119
Fawcett's Bank, 119
Ferguson, Kenneth, 56
ferries, 27,100
financial failures, 119
financial institutions, 72,119
Finch, David W., 40
Finch, George, 40
Finlay, Ann, 120-121
Finlay, Ralph S., 120-121
fire departments, 37
firefighting, 37
fires, 28,84,118
First Nations, 9
Fisher, Jack, 112
fishery, 73
fishing, 107
flax, 60
Fleck, Emily, 47
Fleming, Charles, 112
Florence, 35,51,76,99
flour, 76
fog, 117
football, 111-113
Ford Motor Company, 108
foreign driller, 69,84
Forest, 17,32,37-38,40,59,61,68,77,79
Forest Basket Company, 77
forest products, 59,75,91
forests, 16,18-19,24,32,59,75
Fort du Luth, 8
Fort St. Joseph, 8
forwarding trade, 89
Foulds, James, 40
Fowler, Samuel P., 40
Fraleigh, Howard, 60
Fraleigh, Sid Sr., 60
France, Red, 113

fraternal lodges, 46
French, 8-9,12,23-24,26
French Regime, 8
Froomfield, 84,90,105
funerals, 49

Galinée (explorer), 8
gaol, 39
garbage collection, 37
Gardiner, Joseph, 110
gas, 86
gasoline, 105
Geary, Jim, 113
Geerts, 64
George III, 9
Georgian Bay, 75
Gibb, Jessie, 47
Gibb, Mrs. J., 47
Gibb, Mrs. R., 47
Gibb, Tena, 47
Gibson, Bill, 50
Gilbert, W.H. (ship), 117
Gimli, Manitoba, 92
Girl Guides, 109
Goderich, 17,90
Goldsmith, Charles, 110
Good Templars, 54
Gore of Camden, 18
Gore of Chatham, 23
government, 36-43
Graham, T., 64
grain, 60,76,93,117
grain elevators, 93
Grand Bend, 17,33,57,108
Grand Trunk Railway, 27,32-33,61,92,101-103
Grange, 46
Great Depression, 76
Great Lakes, 87-97
Great Storm of 1913, 96-97
Great Western Railway, 30,34-35,101,103
Green, Harry, 78
Grey, Lord, 15
Grey County, 16
Grey Cup, 113
grieving, 49
Griffin, Myrtle, 47
Griffon (ship), 8
grocery, 65
Guelph, 17
Guernsey, 23
guns, 120-122

Hadden, George A., 70
Hair, Amy, 38
Hair, Jim, 38
Hales, C., 116
Hall, Bill, 113
Hall, Samuel, 40

Hamilton, 81
Hamilton, Andrew, 40
Hamilton, H.W., 78
Hamilton Alerts, 112
Hamilton Hotel, 52
Hamilton Wanderers, 112
Hamonic (ship), 95-96,118
Hand, Charles, 54
Hands, James, 40
harbours, 89-93,95,99
Hard Oilers, 83,84
hardware merchant, 69
Hardy, Mrs. G., 47
Harkness, Mrs. K., 47
Harkness, William G., 40
Harris, Claude, 113
Harsen's Island, 93
Hart, Samuel, 40
Hartigan, Jack, 112
Hartley, J, 64
harvesting techniques, 62
Hayes, Alex, 113
haying, 62
Hayne Milling Company, 74,75
hearses, 49
Hedgewick, Mike, 113
hemp, 60
Henderson, Jim, 78
Henderson, Lorne C. Conservation Area, 41
Henderson, Lorne Charles, 41
Henry, Warren T., 54
Heuser family, 51
Highway 407, 99
highways, 99,108
Hillsborough, 108
Hitchcock, Samuel, 40
Hitchcock family, 73
Hobson, Joseph, 102
hockey, 111
Hogg, Grace, 13
hold-up, 122
Holden, James, 40
holidaying, 107-08
Holley, Alexander F. (ship), 93
Holmes, Moore and Courtright, 28
horse dentists, 98
horseshoing, 98
Hossie, Mrs., 47
hotels, 52,54,107
household fashion, 45
Howard, Dyer, 40
Howard, Tilton, 40
Howden, Samuel, 40
Howe, C.D., 85
Howye, Alexander, 40
Huff, Solomon, 40
Huron County, 33
Huron Tract, 17

Huron Village, 27
Huronic (ship), 94-96
Hutchinson, Mrs. E., 47
Hutchinson, Mrs. G., 47
Hutchinson, Mrs. J., 47
Hyde, Captain George, 12

Icelanders, 92
immigration, 9-13,16-35,92
Imperial Oil, 51,81,84-85
imperialism, 8,9
Impett, Isaac, 40
Independent Order of Foresters, 46
Independent Order of Oddfellows, 46
industrial statistics, 32,84
industry (also see under municipality names)
industry, 21,23,26-28,73-88,91-92,105,115
Ingram, Alexander Jr., 40
ink, 34
insurance, 46,72
intemperance, 39,53
inventions, 80
Inwood, 28
Ipperwash, 108
Ipperwash (Camp), 9
Ireland/Irish, 11,16,39

Jackson, William H., 40
Jacob Lawrence and Sons, 74-75
jail, 39
Japanese military conquest, 85
Johnston, Edward H., 13
Johnston, Mrs. J., 47
Johnston, Sutherland, 13
Johnston, Dr. Thomas G., 13
Johnston, Dr. Thomas W., 13
Johnston family, 45
Jones, E.A., 40
Jones, Henry, 73
journalism, 71

Keating, 71
Kelly, Dan, 78
Kent County, 14,18,70,86,119
Kerby, Duncan M., 40
Kerby, Garnet, 110
Kerr, Elmer, 110
Kerr, Ken, 112
Kerr, Mrs. S., 47
Kerr, Willie, 113
Kettle Point, 40,108
Kettle Point Reserve, 9
Kewley, Mrs. F., 47
Kewley, Gordon, 47
Kewley, Lottie, 47
Kewley, Stuart, 47
Kincardine, 90
Kindall, Thomas, 40

King, Fred, 78
Kingston, 42,112
Kingston Penitentiary, 120
Kingstone, Arthur, 87
Kingstone, Charles, 87
Kinsley, Thomas, 40
Kleinsmith, Elmer, 118
Knight, William J., 110
Knights of Columbus, 46
Knights of Maccabees, 46
Knights of Pythias, 46
Kocot, Casimir, 57
Korvemakers, 64

La Salle, René-Robert, 8
labour unions, 46
Lackie, Bruce, 112
lacrosse, 111
Lake Huron, 8,10,73,75,90,93,107-108,117
Lake St. Clair, 93
Lake Superior, 92,97
Lake Winnipeg, 92
Lakehead, 92
Lakeview Cemetery, 42
Lamb, Jennie, 47
Lambton, John George, 15,29
Lambton County Council, 39,55
Lambton Creamery Company, 79,84
Lambton Farmers' Mutual Fire Insurance Company,
    72
Lambton Mutual Insurance Company, 72
Lambton Scott Act Association, 54
Lambton Shield, 71
Lambton-Kent Creamery, 79
Lanark County, 22,89
land speculators, 20,27
land surrenders, 9
Lapier, Peter, 40
Laurier, Wilfrid, 48,56
law, 36,40
lawn bowling, 111
Laycock, Bill, 50
Laycock, Ham, 50
Leckie, Edith, 47
Leckie, Hazel, 47
Leckie, Mildred, 47
Leckie, Mrs. N., 47
Leckie, Mrs. T., 47
Leckie, Mrs. W., 47
Lee, George H., 40
leisure, 106-113
Les Chutes, 26
Liberal Party, 42
Lillywhite, Fred, 50
Lindsay, N., 110
Linsay, Jonathan, 40
liquor inspectors, 52
liquor smuggling, 57

livestock, 61
lobby groups, 46
Locke, J.T., 66
lodges, 46
London, 34-35,43,69,71,79,84
Lord Durham's Report, 15
Loyal Orange Order, 46
Loyalists, 9,16
lumber, 75
lunacy, 120

Macdonald, John A., 42,52
Mackenzie, Alexander, 39,42,54,71
Mackenzie, Charles, 114
Mackenzie, James, 114
Mackenzie, John, 40
Mackenzie, Robert, 114
Mackenzie, William Lyon, 12
Macklem, Dr. Samuel, 65
mail services, 43
Maitland, Alvin, 78
Maitland, Sir Peregrine, 24
Majestic (ship), 96
Malcolm, Eliakim, 19
manufacturing (also see industry), 73-88
maple sugar/syrup, 59
Marine City, Michigan, 52,56,100
marine history, 89-97,100
markets, 37
Marquette, Michigan, 97
marriage, 45
Marsh, John, 63
Marshall, William J., 40
Marshall family, 44
Martin, Gavin, 40
Martin, Thomas, 40
Marysville, Michigan, 107
Mason, Thomas, 40
Masons, 46
Massucci, Art, 113
material progress, 50
Maxwell, D.A., 105
McAlpine, Daniel, 40
McAuley, Margaret, 47
McAuley, Mrs. P., 47
McCallum, Peter D., 52
McCrae, J.G., 54
McCulloch, Captain, 117
McDonald, John D., 40
McDougall, ?, 56
McElheron, William, 40
McGowan, Ted, 112
McGregor, Jean, 47
McKay, John T., 40
McKelvie, James, 40
McKeown, Marie, 40
McKeune, ?, 78
McLachlan, ? (2), 38

McLachlan, Jessie, 38
McLachlan, Mac, 38
McLachlan, Margaret, 38
McLaren, Hugh, 40
McLaren, W.P., 34
McLean, H.G., 110
McLean, Jack, 113
McLean, John, 38
McLeay, Margaret, 44
McLeay, Tena, 44
McLennan, Mrs. J., 47
McMullen, Dave, 112
McPhedran, George, 112
McQuien, Alex, 112
McQuien, Murray, 112
McRitchie, Hazel, 47
McRitchie, Irene, 47
McWatters, Arnie, 113
meal, 76
meat-packing, 61,77
media, 68,71
medicines, 65,68
Megg, Charles, 40
memorial cards, 49
merchants, 59,65-69,76,91,114
Merritt, P.W. and Son, 91
metallurgy, 80
Methodists, 53
Michigan Central Railway, 103
middle class, 44-45
Middlesex County, 70,119
Midland, Michigan, 85
milk, 61,78-79
milk delivery, 79
Miller, Robert, 40
Milliken, Edna, 47
Milliken, Maud, 47
Milliken, Mrs. O., 47
Milliken, Roberta, 47
mills, 28-30,33,35,60,74-76,88
Mills, Nelson, 107
Minielly, William, 40
Mitchell, John, 40
Molyneaux, ?, 110
Montgomery, Robert, 40
Montreal, 76
Moore (village), 43
Moore, Bill, 50
Moore, C.H., 28
Moore, Cal, 113
Moore, Grace, 47
Moore, Mrs. J., 47
Moore Agricultural Society, 106
Moore Reserve, 9
Moore Township, 12-14,19,21,23,27-
    28,51,53,59,63,86,88,106
Mooretown, 27,43,87
Mooretown Salt Company, 88

Morgan, James D., 40
Moulton, Clark, 45
Mounties, 92
Mowat, Oliver, 54
Mowbray, Mrs. J., 47
Municipal Act of 1849, 20-21,23
municipal development, 8-35,76,81,84-85,89-90,99,108
municipal organization (also see municipalities), 14,16-35
municipal services, 36,37
murder, 120-121
Murray, Ethel, 47
Murray, Mrs. D., 47
music, 110
Myers, Henry J., 40

Napoleonic Wars, 12
natural gas, 86
Nesbitt, Mrs., 47
New France, 8,9
New Zealand, 78
newspapers, 71
Nightingale, Florence, 35
nitroglycerine, 83,115
Noble, John D., 82
Noronic (ship), 95-96
Norris, Ike, 113
North Carolina, 119
North Lambton (City of), 17,32-34
North West Transportation Co., 92
Northern Navigation Co., 92,94-96,118
Norwich, 78
Nova, 85

Oaklands, 12
oil, 19,30-31,69,71,81-87,99
Oil City, 103
oil refineries, 81-82,84-85,90,105
Oil Springs, 30-31,65,71,79,81,86,99,122
Oil Springs Chronicle, 71
Olive Branch (ship), 89
Omar D. Conger (ship), 107
Ontario Natural Gas Storage and Pipelines, 86
Ontario Prohibitory League, 54
Ontario Provincial Police, 40,122
Ontario Rugby Football Union, 112-113
Ontario Street, 99
Ontario Temperance Act, 56,57
Opium and Narcotics Control Act, 60
Ottawa Rough Riders, 113
Oxford County, 78

Paris International Exhibition, 87
Park, Shubal, 18
parks, 17,37,88
Parsaca, Rocky, 113
Parsons, Cliff, 113

patent rights, 80
patriotism, 48,109
Patrons of Industry, 46
Patterson, Gord, 113
pavilions (dancing), 107
Peat, Con, 112
Peninsular War, 21,24,29
Penny Magazine, 11
Pepper, Jack, 110
Perkins, Frank, 112
Perry, 71
Petro-Canada, 105
Petrolea Topic, 71
Petrolia (Petrolea), 31,37-38,40-41,44,46,48,56,69,71,79,81-84,90,103,105,110,112-116
Petrolia Advertiser, 71
Petrolia Bridge Company, 84
Petrolia Citizens' band, 110
Petrolia High School, 112
Petrolia Pork Packing Company, 84
Petrolia Torpedo Ltd., 115
Petrolia Wagon Works, 84,93
pharmacy, 65,68
Phelan, John, 98
photography, 70
picnic grounds, 107
Pine Hill, 33
Pinery Provincial Park, 17
pioneering, 58
Plank Road, 99
Plympton Township, 12,14,22,25,32,43,53,64
Plympton-Wyoming (Town of), 22
Point Edward, 27,33,40,43,73,92-93,95,101,114,117-118
police services, 37,40,54,92,122
politics, 12-13,15,26,41-42,71
Pollard, Bloss, 112
Polymer, 85
Polysar, 85
Port Franks, 87,90,108
Port Huron, Michigan, 8,107,114,117
Port Lambton, 29,43,93,101
Port Sarnia (see Sarnia)
port economies, 89-95
post offices, 30-32,43
postcards, 70
Poussett, P.T., 40
Powell, Donelda, 38
Powell, Melvin, 38
Powell, Miss, 47
Prairies, 92
Presbyterians, 53
Price, James, 40
prime ministership, 42
prisoners, 39,40
prohibition, 53-57
prohibition plebiscite, 56

public morals, 36
Purdy Fisheries Ltd., 73,118

Queen's Park, 41

Radical Jack, 15
railway stations, 103,109
railways, 27-29,39,32-35,61,73,92-93,101-103
Rainsberry, Jack, 112
Rankin, Charles, 22
Rapids (The), 26
Ravenswood, 79
Rebellion (1837), 12,15
Reece's Corners, 105
Regina Roughriders, 113
registry offices, 39
Reilly, Philip, 106
religious revival, 53
reservations, 9
residences, 12,45,64
responsible government, 15
retailing, 59,65-69,76,91,105,114
Richardson, Ben, 78
Riddell, Lillas, 116
Rippin, A.C.H., 110
road building, 99,100
road maintenance, 37,99,100
roads, 10,22,25,71,99,108
robbery, 122
Robertson, James, 40
Robertson, William, 40
Rogers, Charles H., 88
Rose, George, 112
Roy, William, 40
Royal Military College, 112
Royal North-West Mounted Police, 92
Royal Proclamation, 9
rubber, 85
rugby football, 112-113
Rügen (Baltic island), 34
rum running, 57
Russell, George, 51
Russell, John, 51
Rutter, Len, 113
salt, 87,88
Samiel (The), 71
Sanderson, H.L., 110
Sands, Mabel, 47
Sandwich, 43
Sarnia, 12-14,23,26,27,31,34,37-40,42-43,45,49,51-52,54-55,70-71,75-76,79,80,84-89,94-96,98,101-103,105,112-114,117,120-121
Sarnia Bay, 88-89,93,117
Sarnia Collegiate Institute and Technical School, 113
Sarnia Imperials, 113
Sarnia Observer, 120
Sarnia Reserve, 9
Sarnia Township, 14,23,21,26,47,51,53,86,99,104

Sarnia Woollen Mills Company, 76
Sarnia-Lambton Act, 21
Saronic (ship), 96
Saunders, Isaiah, 40
Savage, John, 40
scandals, 119-121
Scarsbrook, Tom, 56
school systems, 38
schools, 38
Schram, Benjamin, 40
Scotland/Scottish, 12,22,16,39,42
Scott Act (see Canada Temperance Act)
Scott, Bessie, 116
Scott, James, 40
secret ballot, 42
Sergeant, Richard, 110
services stations, 105
settlement, 9-13,16-35,58,108
Seven Years' War, 9
sewers, 37,107
Shawanoe Tract, 9
sheep, 61,76
Shell Oil, 90
Shepardson, G.M., 67
Shepherd, Mrs., 47
Shepherd, William, 40
Shetland, 76
ships, 8,89,91,93-97,100,117-118
shooting oil wells, 83
Short, John, 40
sidewalks, 37
Sifto Salt, 88
Silverwood's, 79
Sim, Mrs. A., 47
Sim, Flora, 47
Simpson, Hugh, 112
Simpson, Joseph, 40
Simpson, William M., 40
sin, 53
Sinclair, A.E., 51
Skinner, George, 62
Skinner, James, 62
Skinner, John, 62
Slaight, Benjamin, 40
Slater, James, 40
Slocum, Abraham, 40
Slocum, John P., 73
Smart, David, 33
Smith, Charles, 40
Smith, Frank, 112
Smith, George, 40
Smith, Harry, 112
Smith, Henry B. (ship), 97
Smith, Samuel, 16,20
Smith, William, 120-121
social customs, 44,45,64
social expectations, 44,45
social organizations, 46,47,109

social outlooks, 50,63,109
social roles, 13,52,66
social status, 44,45,64
social structure, 44
Sombra (village), 29,67,97,100
Sombra Township, 14,18,21,23,53-54,120-121
Sons of Temperance, 54
Southworth, Nelson, 33
sports, 109,111-113
St. Andrew's Society, 46
St. Clair Agricultural Society, 106
St. Clair County, Michigan, 102
St. Clair River, 8,11-12,23,27,29,43,51,57,59,89,
    91,93,100-102,107,117-118
St. Clair Township, 21,23
St. Clair Tunnel, 102
St. George's Society, 46
St. Patrick's Society, 46
St. Thomas, 101
Stag Island, 93,107
Standard Oil, 84
Steadman, Mrs., 47
Stevenson, Ken, 113
Stewart, James, 40
Stirling, Bummer, 113
Stokes, Sam, 112
Stoney Point Reserve, 9
storekeepers, 59,65-69,76,91
storms, 96,97,114
Stratford, 17,33,101
street lighting, 37
street paving, 37
Sunnyside, 67
Supreme Court of Canada, 42
surveying, 10,16-35
Sutherland, Grace, 13
Sutherland, Thomas, 13
swamps, 16,19
Sydenham River, 76,100
Syer, A.J., 76
Symington, Alexander, 40
Symington, James, 40
Symington, Thomas Jr., 40

Talbot, Colonel Thomas, 20
Tashmoo Park, 93
Tavener, H.G., 116
taverns, 106
Taylor, Clayton, 110
Taylor, Sylvia, 47
Taylor, Mrs. T., 47
Taylor, William, 110
teachers, 38
teetotalism, 53,89
telephones, 107
temperance, 53-57,89
temperance societies, 46,54
Texas, 86

Thamesville, 70
Thedford, 17,33,74-76,78
Thetford, Vermont, 33
Thom, David, 80
Thomas, Ben, 112
Thompson, Matthew, 40
Thompson, Walter, 110
Thompson, Wesley R., 110
Thompson, William J., 110
Thornton, J.C., 110
Thorpe, Bob, 113
threshing, 62
Thunder Bay, 92
Tillett, J., 110
toll gates, 99
Tontine Drug Store, 65
tornado, 114
Toronto, 42,76,99,101
Toronto Argonauts, 113
tourism, 17,33,107-108
Townsend, Asa, 17,34
trade cards, 68
transportation (also see automobiles, ferries, railways,
    ships, etc.), 77,89-105
treaties, 9
Treaty of Paris, 9
trials, 55,120-122
Trimbel, George, 40
Truan, Joseph, 40
Truan, Robert, 110
Truan, Thomas, 110
Trusler, Alvah, 40
trustees, 38
Tuck, Mrs. G., 47
Turnbull, Bessie, 47
Turnbull, Edith, 47
Tweedsmuir Histories, 47

Union Gas, 86
United Kingdom Alliance, 54
United States, 10,57,76,101
Uttoxeter, 80,98

Valcartier (ship), 96
Van Tuyl, Benjamin, 69
Van Tuyl and Fairbank, 69
VanHorne, Neil, 113
Venning, Thomas, 62
Venning, William, 62
veterinarians, 98
Victoria, Queen, 27,48
Victoria Hall (Petrolia), 37,46
Vidal, Alexander, 54
Vidal, Captain A.T.E., 12
Vidal, Captain Richard Emeric, 12,43
Vidal family, 26
violence, 54

Wake, Walter, 40
Wallaceburg, 79
Walpole Island, 9,21,23,40,57
wardenship, 41
Warwick, Earl of, 16,25
Warwick (village), 10,43
Warwick Township, 14,22,25,32,34,51,53,
    62,64,72,78,87
water systems, 37,107
Watford, 25,34,38,44,72,75-76,78-80,105,119
Watford Agricultural Implement Works, 80
Waugh, ?, 44
Waugh, Emily, 44
Wawanosh, David B., 70
weather, 114,117
Weaver farm, 62
Webb, Bob, 112
Webb, John, 112
Webster, William D., 40
Wellington, Mark, 40
Wellington Roller Mills, 76
Werden, Mrs., 47
Western Canada, 92
Western District, 9,14
Wheeler, Henry, 40
White Rose (trade name), 105
Whitsett, Joseph, 40
Wickware, Jack, 113
Widder, 33
Widder Station, 33
Wilkesport, 52
Williams, James Miller, 30,81
Williams, John, 40
Wilson, W.B., 110
Windlow, John, 65
Windsor, 34,43,118
women in business, 65
Women's Institute, 47
women's organizations, 47
wood products, 59,75,77,91
Woodcock, Joe, 113
woolen mills, 76
Wright, Captain Alfred Montgomery, 96
Wright, Captain William E., 12
Wyoming, 22,30,48,76,79,114,119
Wyoming Woolen Mills, 76
Wyseman, Bob, 113

Young, Mrs. R., 47
youth, 109

Zone Township, 14,20